Dear Mike

Val told Lisa and I about how you're doing and the difficulties, potentially, that could lay ahead.

So we found this and hope it comforts you as only God can.

" And my God shall supply all you need according to His riches in glory by Christ Jesus. "

Phil 4:19

Sincere regards to a terrific fellow.

Keith & Price 4/08

MW01593929

"I'll start with the Caesar, also, and I'll have the angus ribeye, with frites."

"How do you want that prepared?"

I could barely hear him; it was great.

Emma looked at him like he had three heads.

"Medium rare," she said. But it sounded to me like: "Hey, Croissant Boy, do the words Blitzkrieg / Paris / I surrender, mean anything?"

"And you, sir?"

He had to tap me on the shoulder to get my attention because I was just staring at him, with a smile that *showed about 80 teeth.*

"I'll have another martini and the same thing my daughter is having."

When the dinner was over, Rillette Boy brought the check … to my son. I slept like a baby that night. It was one small victory in our war with France. My babies clearly deserve the medals. Gloating was more than enough for me; worked better than Ambien.

We rolled out of the restaurant with Beaujolais Boy just about brushing me off with a whisk broom like they do in fancy men's restrooms. I tipped the guy pretty good (Alex filled out the bill) because I'm not a vindictive person and don't really hate the French. It's actually somewhere more on the level of loathe, but short of hate. A fine line, to be sure, and one they cross frequently just by their mere existence. It's their arrogance I don't get. They think America should be kissing their bottoms in Macy's window. Us of all people? If we hadn't been involved intimately in their recent history, they'd be holding Bund meetings at the Eiffel Tower as I write this. As a way of thanks to them, I'm going to write a book about French loyalty.

OK, I'm done.

Like DeGaulle said, how can you get along with people in a country where they have 400 kinds of cheese? I couldn't have said it better myself.[xiv] This one's for you, Chuck!

My babies brought me breakfast the next day. We set off to see the sites, with a stop at the National World War II Memorial, the Vietnam Veterans Memorial, and the Lincoln Memorial.

National World War II Memorial

I was prepared to be overwhelmed and was completely … underwhelmed. It, and I really hate to say it, sucked. It was … nothing. The only truly moving aspect of it was the memorabilia folks left at various spots. If you want to burst with pride while at the same time crying your eyes out, just read that stuff. I thought of my uncle who was in the first wave at Omaha. I thought of a bloke I ran into at York Minster, I think it was, who was reading from the "Book of the Dead" from World War 2. These were men (the Royal Yorkshiremen, in this case, I believe) with whom he clearly had fought and was trying to remember; saying their names out loud and crying. That is an experience I'll *never* forget.

Vietnam Veterans Memorial

When I saw the VVM years ago, I was insulted by it. At that time, the sentiment was echoed by a bunch of vets. Over time, I've grown to love it, and so have most of them. I very much lived through that era but wasn't drafted because the war was winding down. It was a good, just, and moral war. And we can't be criticized for its undertaking. I'd also venture to say that the three million people the Commies killed after we left would be inclined to agree with me. Those victims knew who the real enemy was, no matter how we always try to "spin" it today.

The Lincoln Memorial

My kids liked hanging out at the Lincoln Memorial. I told them how I thought President Lincoln really had his work cut out for him. He simply wouldn't let the Union split. It was treason, and the Union was too important to ever be allowed to dissolve. Lincoln knew that, though I'm not sure I would have. His character and wisdom have been a barometer against which I've always measured myself. Yes, I admire him that much. This being high praise ... from a Copperhead.

I also don't know if I would have been quite as magnanimous in my policies after the war was done. I may have pretended the Rebels were French and started executing people. Cooler heads prevailed, and thank God for that. Please note I'm not without good company in my thinking overall. When the war in Europe was over, Churchill – another of my idols – wanted to find Nazis, prove it, and put them up against the nearest wall. If it took ten seconds from discovery to execution, then so be it. No mercy. I happen to agree with him. Maybe in one instance this policy would have been right; in the other, wrong. Nuremberg dragged out for years, and I believe we learned very little from it. Maybe executions, at once and immediate, would have been better. Over 30 million people dead? That's quite enough for me, thank you, to start killing people. How about a hundredth of that figure? Let's be honest: even Jesus couldn't forgive those Nazi vermin.

It was time to eat, before going to Arlington, which is one of my favorite spots on this earth. We went to an Italian restaurant. The waiter was a little impatient, and so was the host. I started drawing conclusions that may or may not have been warranted: Is this a French thing? A Washington thing? Did I have a re-elect Bush lapel pin on my shirt? *What?*

So, the maître d' seats us outside, and then it takes the waiter, "Mr. Tajikistan," about ten minutes to take the drink order. I am starting to get a little torked, but not enough to make a scene ... yet. I apparently have another wagon to fix.

Is this starting to sound familiar in any way?

So, "Attitude Boy" comes back. We order drinks, he gives us menus, and I steal a glance at his name tag. It was the kind of name that has no vowels, OK? All right, I'm exaggerating a little. There may have been one vowel. I'm personally starting to get, rightly or wrongly, an attitude that I, Keith J. Price, "am a citizen and you ain't" syndrome. But I wasn't going to act on it ... yet. I've ripped people new ones before for less, but I'm much better now, thank you.

My kids ordered Salade niçoise.

Oh, if only you had been there to see the look on "Uzbekistan's" face; yet another photo for the Smithsonian. We finished, he started the whisk broom number on me (with his wagon appropriately fixed), and I felt pretty darn good.

The putz.

I should note that while all this is going on during the day before and in this instance, my oldest misses some of it. I have to explain, nicely, to her, why I'm getting a little miffed. In other words, I have to go through it a second time. I get impatient about doing this after a couple of times, then get cranky. I get a mamaluke waiter who's been placed by cosmic fate, within my path from point A to point B, and I'm ready to call out Mr. Lincoln's troops and have myself a nice little war. I can say quite a lot, without actually having to verbalize; a little intimidation, if you will. But I use it sparingly, except with some arrogant waiter or desk clerk who comes from some dirt pile, to our American sanctuary, and *has attitude*. The "IAAACAYA" starts to take hold, and I begin to lose my poise, what little I already have. A schmuck from a major airline is still feeling whether he has a behind after I got through with him. I forgot, for the moment back then, that "dipstick" could have had me arrested for security reasons. But he insulted my wife. You go straight to execution if you do that in my presence; no jury, no trial, no lawyers, just one deadly punch in the face.

I told his supervisor, who subsequently did a nice little number on him herself. God is good.

Anyway, what I was saying is that Em is an extremely perceptive child with the ability to read lips at a distance. You wouldn't believe the stuff she reports to me, like the things people say, especially when they're trying to go further than a kiss goodnight. Her current boss has her reading the lips of the patrons at his restaurant to know what they're saying. Her lip reading ability is a wonderful asset for me and her mom to use nefariously, until the goofy ACLU decides to sue me for invasion of privacy. Wouldn't surprise me. But anyway, sometimes my baby doesn't know what's happening two feet away. It's a terrible way to live.

On our battlefield trek, before Arlington, the last field we visited was Manassas National Battlefield Park. Once again we drove through some gorgeous country to get there, but I must say the closer we got, the countryside became more densely populated. And with that came the visual overload of shopping centers, restaurants, and service stations. It was at this moment, and would be something I'd decide unequivocally before returning to Texas, that our plans to retire to this part of the country were thereby axed. It was less a thought than a feeling, at this point, but I was aware of something amiss.

We wended our way to the battlefield. It was drizzling and then stopped abruptly. The weather patterns we experienced on this trip were consistent: rain, then sun, then rain, then sun. Sort of like a baptism followed by absolution, if one really wanted to read into it. At this point in my life, I was ready to look for signs no matter how absurd they might appear. However, I thought these had more than a little merit. People have been writing about these cycles as metaphor, after all, for centuries. But OK, maybe not the Virginia variety.

When we got out of the car, my son said my tire was making noise. The noise was similar to what the "Arabs of lore" would make, particularly after enjoying some roasted lamb. I say folkloric because I spent several years in the Middle East and never had the pleasure of experiencing the result of that specific body function, coming from someone who uses a stick to brush their teeth. And I thank God I was out of the country before they let one of those rip. Must have smelled like New Jersey.

We didn't get to really see Manassas and, I'm sure, a wonderful electric map. We went to a tire store and they labored for *90 minutes* trying to remove the object from the tire. A nail? No. A chunk of wood? No. A busted valve? No.

It was an animal bone.

I'm pretty sure it was the remnants of a dead animal, since I don't recall running over a living one. It was a huge undertaking to get out. They really labored to get the thing free of the tire. But finally they did, and I tipped them handsomely. Then I started to think about that turtle and that maybe he was involved in some way. "Honey, it took me an hour to get half way across the road and some liberal PITA PETA member put me back where I started. I'll get that Yankee, if it's the last thing I ever do" (rebel yell). And so he did, my friends, and so he did.

Arlington National Cemetery

Arlington is one of my favorite spots on earth. It was JFK's also, which means there was something appealing in its majesty. It could simply have been the view from the Custis-Lee Mansion. I don't know.

For anyone who hasn't been there, it's a solemn place. To me, the fact that they still observe, to the letter, original traditions (i.e. the changing of the Guard) keeps the continuity of our culture intact and represents the very best we have to offer as a nation. I believe, and have preached to my kids, that tradition is not the bad thing people seem to say it is. I personally, don't want to change a darn thing about our lives here in America. OK, maybe some minor tweaking, but after all, we're the greatest country on earth; the most compassionate, collectively, in the majority; God-fearing; and we are, simply, on the side of right.

Period.

I believe, at the time of this writing, my beloved country is in trouble. This attitude gets crystallized when I visit places like Arlington, and I need to reassure myself that there are foundations at hand that can sustain me while I go through – what would you call it? – this current "mind squeeze." As far as this country, God blessed this endeavor, and we are the closest thing to His intentions on earth. Call me silly, but I actually believe this stuff. Elders are to be respected; marriage is a sacred institution; our leaders, at their core, genuinely care; we respect our boss and put the company above ourselves; clean humor and language are actually good things (I wish I practiced what I preached, but I *am trying* to be funny); sensitivity to others, like when they are brutally murdered, is not turning the page since this was a *life* we're talking about here. The military is an honorable profession deserving of total respect; and there are clearly enemies of our Judeo-Christian nation who are genuine haters, beyond rehabilitation, that have to be eliminated by any means at hand. And sometimes our youth have to die while eliminating these enemies. And none of them has died for naught, contrary to what the *New York Times* says and has been saying for 50 years. None. We are noble and basically unselfish; with an uncommon sense of fairness that permeates everything we do. Our Founding Fathers were religious and knew, *I mean knew*, that none of our greatness could come from anyone other than God. And they were, possibly, smarter than anyone ever was. Even me.

Simply put, we're everything the French aren't. And this, also, is a good thing. Arlington never fails to make me cherish what I have and, most importantly, what brought us to where we are.

About 20 years ago, maybe more, I had some time off between jobs, and I decided to make a field trip. I drove back to Pennsylvania for a ten-year high school reunion and stopped in DC on the way home. I went to Arlington and was casually walking around behind the amphitheater, after putting out my cigarette. I was a chain smoker in those days, and the Arabs taught me to take it to new consumption levels later. I looked down as I was walking, and I thought I was hallucinating. I was looking at the headstone of Audie Murphy, the most decorated soldier of WW2.

Here lay, I think it's safe to say, one of the bravest guys who ever lived. Several medals, including the Medal of Honor, for personally killing something like a battalion of Germans, were listed on the headstone. And he had no special marker whatever. It was just another tombstone in a long row of stones throughout all of Arlington. The only characteristic that made his stone a little different was the cross at the top emblazoned in gold, meaning Medal of Honor. I was amazed and humbled by the inconspicuousness of the whole thing. I went through the litany of brave deeds Murphy had done when I visited with the kids, until they were of the same mindset as I: there are genuine heroes in this country. We have folks who don't need their seamy underside, if it exists, examined ad nauseum. God forbid we should actually admire someone and leave it that way. What the heck is wrong with us? This is a question I have to ask.

On this trip with the kids, as I came up to the spot where Murphy was buried, I pointed out the headstones of the famous military men: Admiral Leahy (Chief of Naval Operations), Arthur MacArthur (whose son Douglas you may have heard of, and Arthur himself, a ridiculously brave little lad at Missionary Ridge), Claire Chennault (of Flying Tigers fame and my neighbor's cousin), President Taft, to name a few. All of whom would have been required to salute Audie Murphy because he won the Congressional Medal of Honor. Very cool. And I know I keep saying it, but all Audie had was that little government issue headstone. Had that been me, at the very least, I would have had a small, well-lit … billboard. But it's their personal qualities that make genuine heroes. And thank God for it; we're a better country because we have people like that.

The Land of Tolls and Taxes

Our next move was to Atlantic City and visit my dad, the kid's "Poppy." My dad passed away while I was writing this book, but he lived a good 90 years. My dad and I didn't really know each other too well for many years. In his defense, I'll say he was a Depression Era kid, one of 13, who had to scramble and hustle to make a living. After years of perseverance he hooked up with After Six in 1955. At that time, After Six owned the formal wear business as a manufacturer. He was a straight commission guy who, in the 60s, began to make serious money. With that, we moved to the suburbs and into a nice house with all the trappings of the almost well-heeled. This was the period when I spent the elemental parts of my youth. Not a lot of emotional growth, though this came later.

It's worth noting that when my dad started with After Six, he literally asked the owner, Sam Rudofker, to take a chance on him. They came to an agreement about compensation. And here's the part worth noting: Mr. Rudofker asked my dad about his family.

Four kids.

Did his wife work?

No.

What were his bills like?

It would make a lousy balance sheet.

"OK," Mr. Rudofker said, "I don't want you worrying about money while you try to build this territory for us (Minnesota), so here are "x" dollars per week. Get to work."

I'd say this rarely happens any more. My dad spent around 40 years at After Six, and when there was a family squabble or internal power struggle, he sided with Mr. Rudofker. He never made a big deal out of it to me and hardly mentioned it, but the loyalty was there. It became an essential part of my character as well. Loyalty is everything.

As I said before, I didn't know my father too well. When I was young, he gave me everything I ever wanted, but he didn't allow me to get to know him. I discovered later that emotionally, he gave me what he was capable of giving. It would have been unfair to demand he give more than that. This perspective came with maturity. For quite a few years, I made him pay for it and was pretty angry all the time. I followed the lead of other family members who still harbor the resentment. Trauma should get better with time, not worse. If it gets worse, there's generally something wrong with the bearer. I cut my ties with those people, and my relationship with my dad blossomed. I grew up, no one was constantly stirring the pot, and I benefited, my entire family has, by the love that was generated between my dad and my little family. And he also apologized 500 times for divorcing my mom. I didn't ask that he did so; he *chose* to. What more could anyone, with any amount of maturity, possibly ask for? And he apologized the 500 times and not out of convenience. Really, what more? He also did something else, twice.

My dad visited us about six years ago. It was the first long stay together and it would be just us: Lisa, me, the kiddies. The kids spent most of the time slobbering all over him. Remember, this is not a touchy, feely guy, but I didn't see him moving out of the way. I did notice him sucking it up with a straw, however. We fed him, gave him martinis, sat him on the porch, let him hold court, tell jokes, charm the absolute devil out of everyone, and let my kids slobber all over him. All in all, a great couple of days. We acted like we always do. There was lots of love and kisses, between me and Li, hugging on

the babies, eating well, drinking wines of outstanding vin-
tages, and hanging with my neighbors: my perfect life.

As we sat together later in a restaurant in Atlantic City,
my dad expressed his innermost sentiments. I wasn't even
remotely prepared for what I was about to hear, so I ordered
another martini … and hurry please. Paraphrasing, this is
what he said, in his gravelly voice, with food on his shirt (God
love him):

"Keith, I want you to know something. When I visited
you in Dallas, I observed a couple of things. I saw a lot of
love in that house. I saw the interaction, between you and
Lisa. And you with the children. I saw how well brought up
they are. What a wonderful, loving, welcoming place your
home is. I can't tell you how lucky I am to have a son like
you, with your precious family."

At this point, I was crying into my stuffed mushrooms
and drinking like a fish. I was in no way prepared to hear this
heartfelt expression of love and respect. It *rocked my world*. I
was gargling martinis, I was so overwhelmed. It took 86 years
and was well worth the wait. I didn't need to hear it; he simply chose to tell it, in front of people, so I could relish its full
effect.

Then he wrote me a letter telling me how proud he was
of me. That having a son like me was the greatest gift he
could ever have. That God had blessed him beyond reason.
And how much he loved me. I forgot he sent it to me. I found
it in a pile of other letters. I re-read it and cried like a two year
old, as I'm prone to do. I don't think it's possible to love
someone as much as I loved my dad, warts and all. All of
which he was cognizant of. But I don't give a hoot about
those warts.

I loved my mom, too, who was a *real* tigress. Hard to love, most of the time, but I did, and I never gave her up.

I visited him in Florida, where he lived later (all the old tuxedo salesmen go there to die). I took him to dinner at a fancy steak place (Ruth's Chris). He hadn't seen me in a year. I'd lost a ton of weight and was strong as an ox and built like one. We sat at the table. I filled his wife with wine. I filled him with vodka. I may have even had a few myself.

And then he said to me: "Keith," (in his gravelly voice and with food on his shirt), "sometimes I think I failed you as a father."

Geez dad, could you stop throwing me these haymakers? I said to myself.

I spent the next five minutes going over the litany of things he'd done for me: seeing the Beatles live; seeing the *original* Temps at the Copacabana, front row center, like at Henry Hill's table; paying for college; letting me live in a nice house, with food always on the table; nice clothes. "So you weren't huggy / kissy" (his biggest regret). "Well dad, to be honest, that kind of stuff makes me nervous unless I can pre-pare for it … in advance. Even today. So, tell me again how you failed me." It was the best extemporaneous speech I've ever given while under supreme emotional duress. It was at a time when I really needed to do so. I reassured him that he was the best father *any* kid could ask for. I loved him, I told him, more than just about anyone else in my life. It was my pleasure, and my wife's, to support him financially as best we could (he didn't quite expect to live quite this long). And God was good to me for putting me in this position to help and having the wherewithal to do so. And not to worry: he was the best, and I loved him to death for it.

"Do you feel OK now, dad?"

"Yes, I do."

I said that I was glad to be able to reassure him and that he needn't worry. Ever. "Now, enjoy your dinner, OK?"

Two weeks later, he was dead.

This was, essentially, my last substantive conversation with him. And people think there is no God?

If one thinks about it (and I am a relentless thinker), the whole experience begs a larger question: why did I deserve to keep being rewarded like this, having my last real conversation with dad to be one of such simplicity, yet to be so profound in the greater scheme of things? That's genuine love for me that *Someone has.* This love isn't random fate, two atoms coming together in the vast universe and creating this experience. No way is it some haphazard convergence of the ethers, purposeless in their original intent. I don't believe that I, or anyone, with any sense, (if I may speak for them), could buy into fate as the ultimate driving force here or in our lives. Just from this experience, the odds would be dead set against it. But this isn't the only blessing I have, which adds substance to the argument of God's hand in this, my life. I have a loving wife, two great babies, the best dad ever, great in-laws, wonderful and giving friends, a good place to work, a great home in a great state, and despite my travails of late, lucky enough in having this perspective: God has never abandoned me, not for one billionth of a second. Now or ever.

What more in my life, could I or anyone, reasonably request? I'd feel like a charlatan having half of the blessings I enjoy today. But why me, of all people, being so rewarded, a pusillanimous little git currently running for his life in a quest for perspective? I've labored a long time over the years and now, trying to figure this out, I think I may know what it is. I'm compelled to note that I feel presumptuous by guessing.

But here goes (and so much for humility): I never thought about it; it was just there, and deep inside me. I've always intensely and passionately loved God, even when I had no idea how to show it or how to reach Him (as if we had to do such a thing).

Could it really be this simple? I mean, I have to ask. I guess it has to be, because I can think of a million reasons why God wouldn't like me ... *or anyone else*, for that matter. So what possibly supersedes all the human foibles to which we are all fated and allows us to be continually blessed, despite ourselves? Devotion and love for Him is all I've been able to come up with. Possibly we complicate it all too much; the real answer may be a very simple one, like here. Maybe I just love Him, and I use that love as a guide in my life, with this edict being all He asks of me. The rest: window dressing. I was feeling better. Life can be simple, I thought, very simple until people get involved and complicate everything.

But during our road trip, before we could go to New Jersey to see my dad, we had to, of course, drive through Maryland and Delaware. ("Dellawer" to those living there and "Merland.") I noticed something that I found very annoying (what else is new?). My wife and I made plans to consider retiring to this part of the world (it was here or Tahiti, ya' know?). But something dawned on me as I was driving thru it: I didn't like it anymore. Thomas Wolfe was right. Forget the fact they get you coming and going, for everything it seems. The people aren't friendly. They make it seem like you're imposing on them. Not all the people, just the ones in the very important "service industry," where courtesy and manners would be a little appreciated and probably increase business considerably. Instead, we get retired Nazi camp guards. Who needs it on a continual basis? I had my fill of these folks in Philly growing up ... and every time I visited there since.

"I'll have a steak with onions."

"YOUSE WANT CHEESE WIT' THAT?"

"No, plain, with onions. Didn't I just say that?

"NEXT!"

"Merry Christmas, by the way."

I called my bride right then and there. She was a little surprised. But I explained my point. I also didn't want to become one of them. I'm moody enough already. Plus, the place looks worn out and the heck with that. I could look in the mirror if I wanted old and worn out.

After mortgaging my house several times to pay the tolls getting to Atlantic City from DC, we checked into the Tropicana hotel. My babes had never been in a "Casina" before, and this place was really hopping ... at 12 in the afternoon. They were impressed by all the lights and noise and second-rate lounge acts, with some very hard-looking women and hard-looking men staring at them.

No thanks.

But my luck was holding. This older guy checked us in, took a shine to my babies, and asked them if they wanted a room low in the hotel or high. They responded, and he gave us a much better room than I booked, I'm sure. It was the floor below the penthouse, with a view of the ocean. It didn't include the Atlantic's smell, I am happy to report.

He took quite a shine to my babies. He kept track of them for a couple of days. The fact they rode down the elevator early in the morning just to say hello didn't hurt. I'm sure most people abused the guy.

I saw this victim's syndrome later that night when I accidentally wandered into part of the "Casina" with the kids in tow. It was the way the place was configured. Plus I had a couple of drinks with dad, was a little upset at his condition, and was emotional, to say the least. All of a sudden, some Casino guard starts giving me very loud abuse. You should have heard this guy. What a rude ... I proceeded to yell back at this dirtbag, who yelled right back at me. I asked him politely, at the top of my lungs, who the fuck did he think he was talking to, exactly? I'm afraid I used those exact words, in front of my kids. He gave me some more grief, and I really tried to open his descending colon for him, verbally for now but more later, if needed. And then it dawned on me. This putz must get treated like this all the time, or why the attitude over an honest mistake? But enough of his reasons for being a moron. I'm not a liberal, and I spend like zero time wondering why misfits are misfits. I really didn't give the remotest shit, at that moment. My dad worried me, and I was upset. I was in a place I consider to be a major dump, Atlantic City, and now I get attitude from some Hukbalahap? It was too much to deal with short-term and not possible in the long-term. I wasn't God's witness at that precise moment, to be sure. Additionally, I decided right then I was leaving a day early. Forever. And I have no regrets about either decision. I hope God thinks I did right. I may even suggest he does. After all, he didn't create Caspar Milquetoast when he made me.

We went to dinner. While we were waiting for our food, my youngest was played a video trivia game with an older lady at the bar, who loved him. He could answer the questions and get her free drinks, and I couldn't pull him away. I was half expecting him to tell me to shove off; that he was busy making time.

"Now let's have another Manhattan," I pictured him saying, "and talk about you and me, OK sugar?" This went through my mind until I shook it off. The kid scares me.

As we sat there, without my sawed-off version of Rudolf Valentino, I glanced over at my daughter and watched her as she looked at my dad. I leaned over and asked her if she thought her Poppy was cute or what.

"Of course," she said, "he's the cutest."

My daughter is the most loyal relative a person could have. You'd have to prove yourself a complete idiot to lose this loyalty. When my father-in-law lay in a coma, my twelve-year-old daughter stayed at his side holding his hand whenever she could. Not many twelve year olds will do that sort of thing. And I didn't expect her to. She was right there, an immoveable object. She has a gift. She looked at my dad with the same eyes. God, I was proud of her, now and on that other day.

But we had a new problem. Our laundry was stacking up, and I needed to get it done. It was hard to believe, sort of, that a big "Casina" like the Tropicana didn't have a laundry facility. Then again, I believe the whole purpose of the northeast portion of America is to make one's life as complicated as possible. Think about it: go to Philly or New York and tell me something that goes easily, with a minimum of fuss and bother. Even a cup of coffee means they have to spill half the cup down its side before they hand it to you. Now here's the weird part, I love New York City. I just have no expectations of it. I'd even live there, if I had that cool million I keep dreaming about.

What I thought I'd do was get my kids down to the pool, situate them, and take my laundry to the laundromat. It almost worked until I was rudely reminded that I was in New Jersey. Sorry, you can't leave your kids without supervision; *you* have to be the lifeguard. That's the rules. I'd run into the same thing in Philly. Too many rules. Texas isn't like this. The whole life up there is a genuine pain. I was looking at this muscle-bound mook telling me about his rules, and I wasn't sure if oxygen was getting to his brain. He was wearing a sleeveless muscle shirt and sounded like Rocky. He had 300 gold chains and 200 tatts. Very attractive. We had a lot in common, he and I, in that we'd both been in 5th grade, though me only once. I looked for the exit, so I could keep running away from people like this. And to think there's probably some Jersey girl hot for this guy. I don't want to think about the girl. I think I'll throw up now about the state of the world.

I left the kids in our room under orders to not open the door for any reason short of a biblical-style conflagration. I carried the laundry to a laundromat five blocks away. Beautiful place, Atlantic City. Basically anything outside the "Casina" is Beirut. I started doing my laundry, and this guy comes over and introduces himself to me. I looked around a little bit to see who he was talking to. We start "B-S ing" to pass the time. I was glad, because he was teaching me laundromat protocol. Believe it or not, it actually exists, with its own perceptions of decorum (i.e., don't ask for change from the moody old raisin who's supposed to be providing it, and certainly don't tell him the dryers are blowing cold air. He may get angry, having to do his job).

My new best friend told me he was a bus driver for SEPTA, and he was taking a month off, just gambling.

"That sounds terrific,: I said, "I hope you win." I told him, coincidentally, I was from Philly but lived in Texas. "What route do you drive, by the way?"

Now, I don't know about you, but there are few coincidences in this life. My NBF (new best friend) had a bus route that started at Washington Lane, then went down Stenton Avenue through to Lafayette Hill. I was reared within five blocks of that starting location and lived from 7th grade thru college at the end of his route, Lafayette Hill. And here I was washing dirty undies in some fleabag laundromat in Ramadi, and I met one of my kin, so to speak. So what if he was black? He was my bro.

We reminisced about some of the old places I knew very well but weren't there any longer. It had been 40 years since Washington and Stenton for me. He asked me if I knew the Chinese place. I thought he was messing with me. Darn straight, I did.

"It's still there."

"Get the "****" outta here!" (I used a slightly different word, obviously ...)

"No, it's still there, for real."

"No way, it was 50 years old when I started going there!"

It was *still there*. Who could believe it? So, I told him my story.

We were allowed to go home for lunch when I was in elementary school, also still there.xv Sometimes, my mom gave me a dollar to go out to eat. Within 2 blocks of the school, I had several choices about how to spend that dollar: Grilli's, for a cheese steak and a discussion of "Lost in Space" with my friends; Gansky's, for a burger, fries and a Coke (75 cents in those easy times); the drugstore to wait for the latest *MAD* magazine (35 cents), and while waiting, read every comic book they had on the shelves and eat Goldenburg's Peanut Chews, that fabulous, rip out your dental work, candy. Or, if I was bored, I could walk over to the camera store that sold 45s to see the latest stuff they had out. It was the heyday of the Temps, Supremes, etc. One day, I skipped lunch entirely and bought my mom "I Hear a Symphony," I think, from the Supremes. Or I could go to the bowling alley and see those new-fangled comic book dispensers they had to keep us from pilfering and play pinball. Or I could go to my friend's butcher shop and look at the kosher-killed dead chickens. It created a certain morbid curiosity in me, and they tasted great, when cooked.

Or I could go to the Chinese place and have Grace, the waitress, give me a bowl of wonton soup, a giant plate of pork fried rice, an egg roll and all the tea and sugar I could drink … for the outrageous cost of 76 cents, with a dime tip that she was happy to get. And she couldn't wait to see me again, I was considered so generous. She was quite a lovely specimen of the female persuasion, I might add, something I'd come to appreciate later in life, though I wasn't doing too bad a job at 11. I recall very clearly that the owner would come out during lunch and sit with a big plate of ground pork, eggs, and the wonton pastry shells. And he'd sit and make wontons the whole time I was sitting there … while chain smoking over the mound of pork. Yum. Today, he'd be put in prison for doing that. And he used an abacus to figure out my bill. How cool was that? The wontons were delicious, by the way. Smoky.

With the change left over, I could go to the variety store and buy a rubber ball to screw around with or some baseball cards. All of this was within two blocks of my school. I haven't even mentioned the other restaurants or the toy stores or the bank where you could guess the number of peanuts in a giant aquarium and win some cold hard cash. I was all about cash in those days.

I had this "free for all" while growing up. I've been asked if I took the kids to see these places and go in them again. I didn't really, because how could I explain what it meant to me and possibly convey its impact on the happy memories of my childhood that this place helped to create? I drove through and gave them a fleeting glimpse of their dad. They appreciated what I experienced and were even a little jealous of my ability to roam at will. No predators looking for me; not even a hint of that stuff, though we'd heard of it, but not like today.

I had an idyllic childhood, one I wish my kids could have. I know this can't happen any longer, and this is truly regrettable. I worry like crazy about what my kids are exposed to. I think it's a total charade to think of the world as a better place today than before. Look at what I was able to do; it certainly couldn't be duplicated today. I believe the world is a somewhat horrid place on so many levels; worse than before. A clear right and wrong always exists, but the line of delineation for whoever's agenda has blurred even this simple truth. Where's the wholesomeness I remember? Who said life *had* to be coarsened? How did creating a modicum of skepticism and cynicism in my kids, out of necessity, make them better? I had the wholesomeness and none of the worry. I hope what Lisa and I provide is enough. Providing it is really the core of our existence. So, they eat the wheat flakes.

I grew up playing all afternoon and not coming home 'til they were screaming for me to have dinner, rain or shine. I wasn't playing an organized sport every second (usually three at a time) or learning the piano and practicing every second. Or doing all these things every night of the week. I had freedom, and I learned to love it. I didn't take advantage of it, either. I still turned out pretty good. I respected older people, and I wouldn't dream of giving them static. Didn't notice "color" until I was forced to and thought it started and stopped right there. I played chink, wall ball, stick ball, wire ball, step ball, dodge ball, and traded soul records with my friend, Lily. I never studied a lick, having been the city-fied version of Huck Finn. I made the Safety Patrol, ate like a horse, by virtue of my mom being the greatest cook *that ever lived*, watched TV when it was good, and got cultured, in a contemporary way, by my sisters and parents. I thought stealing a beer out of the fridge was a major crime, made out with girls, and thought "going to bed" with them was *getting into bed* with them and being happy just to be there.

By contrast, both bad and good ... first, the Bad. My kids have started to play video games (which Lisa and I hated and prevented them from playing for years), listen to CDs with age ratings on them, and watch cartoons that are mainstream, but make us sick (who are these boors?).

But for a brief moment, the Good. My kids get cultured in the likes of Sinatra, Dean Martin, and Marlon Brando, so they have a brain in their heads.

Then the Bad, again. My kids have the chance to pick up forms of VD that can't be cured but are easily accessible; be exposed daily to impersonal sex like it's eating lunch (thanks to what they see on TV) and do any drug they want, more powerful and addicting than anything I had ever *heard of* as a kid. Now they're creating this stuff in a lab to further their sordid agenda. *Creating it.* Mainstream girls can wear clothes now that only the worst sluts I grew up with would consider wearing. And those that should be stigmatized and are now celebrities can flaunt it and demand acceptance or the heck with you.

So, is the world is a better place today?

Recall, for less than a dollar, I could gorge myself, read comic books, play pinball, eat candy, and have change left. And I didn't live in fear unless I fell over from eating too much and tore the new pants my mom bought me. That, my friends, *is real fear*. Trust me. She was one tough broad who, luckily, loved me or I wouldn't be writing this book. I'd have stumps instead.

But Back to the Issues at Hand, Today's Trip …

We visited my college alma mater, St. Joseph's University. I graduated in 1977. I took a year off to make golf balls on the night shift at a local factory. They liked my work ethic so much they eventually promoted me to sandblaster, with a nickel raise. I'd made the "big time." They had machinery at that plant that created so much heat you could cook meat on the grates. Which I did, by the way, more than once. Delish! I was the Galloping Gourmet while my friends were eating fries. This is really the story of my life, if you think about it.

As we walked around the campus, it was obvious that after all these years, the place had changed dramatically, not the least of which was from going from college to university. But it was still kind of homey. The university rests on the Main Line of Philly, and the old, beautiful houses were used for classrooms and dorms. Not too shabby. It created a warm atmosphere that, in my opinion, the Jesuits created just through their presence and administration of the university. Later, I became disillusioned with the church itself during its child molestation scandals (how they handled them) and some other rigmarole, major and minor. But at that time, and really up through today, the church is always bigger than the folks that run it, thank goodness. And I still attend and love it.

I found God during my stay at St. Joseph's, and I have no regrets whatsoever about my experience. (He found me, of course, but allow me the traditional expression.) St. Joe's, then, was perfect in every way to me. I was really exposed to the realities of ethics and morality; the whole body of

Catholic philosophy. I'm happy to state this core learning experience has never left me and influences most everything I do. I share this experience very frequently with my kids, also. I like to think they, as well as I, have bought into the program totally. Time will tell.

Around the corner from where I had most of my classes was the Barnes Foundation, which houses the largest collection of Renoirs in the world. It's an old mansion. For students, it was free or something like a dollar, I don't remember. Now the foundation's collection tours the world and wows the public. But back then, it was some tiny enclave that no one seemed to know about. I spent many an afternoon in that place getting up close and personal with Impressionist art ... for hours at a time.

My son decided he was going to college at SJ while we walked around. I guess he could do worse (I could never get into the place using their standards today). My wife went to William and Mary, and that place is beyond the pale as far as beauty and historical context are concerned. I'd settle for either one of my kids going there. My daughter is still undecided, but we've mentioned Rice University. How happy would that make us? Our deaf baby getting into such a prestigious university and having the wherewithal to get there. (While I was editing this book, long after the road trip, we visited Washington University, at their request, so Emma could see the campus. Wow.)

After graduation, I moved to California. I worked a couple of jobs, got engaged and happily dis-engaged, met some famous people, entertained my friends doing imitations of them, and ended up in the industry where I toil today. I admit I was getting a little bored. I wanted to see what was "out there." I didn't want to become "The Man in the Gray Flannel Suit" at 23.

After a pretty long effort (about seven years), I joined a firm and became their representative in the Middle East. That place would never be the same, my friends. I'm joking, of course, but I wanted to see the world so badly, routinely, I ended up in a place about which I knew virtually nothing and had even less interest in. But I said why not, and ended up going to Europe after each trip to Saudi, Oman, Jordan, Qatar, UAE, Bahrain, and Kuwait (great Kentucky Fried Chicken; but we should have let Saddam keep it, the people are so irritating).

So, here's the kicker. I totally loved it. I couldn't love a place more. The people were simple, in the most positive way. It was hot, so who wanted complications? That was my personal theory related to their lack of urgency in anything. I learned what selling really meant. At first, they "ate my lunch." They were masters at negotiating lower-level business. Then I became intelligent and *started to eat their lunch* and make some serious money in the process. Life was good, no fundamentalists tried to kill me … yet. I got to see that world I'd been hankering to see, in spades. Here are some of the places I had the fortune to go to: England (loved it, *as you know*), Wales (too quaint to be believed[xvi]), Scotland (nice people, horrible chow[xvii]), Germany (except for the occasional Bundist, my favorite), Denmark (party animals, with great Danish), Austria (except for the occasional Bundist, not too bad), Holland (usually covered in mud and bird poo), northern Italy (gorgeous), Japan (good, except for the occasional *Samarai* Bundist …), China (the nicest, most trusting people I had met to date), Mexico (I've been to the highest, I've been to the lowest, literally and figuratively, and I actually liked the place. When I climbed to the top of the Temple of the Sun, what were they doing? Selling trinkets). Did I miss anything?

OK, so in some respects, I'm considered weird by worldly travel types: I loved Germany, especially Bavaria. When those people aren't killing undesirables, you could grow to love the place. Germany is a very big part of America. The German influence is unavoidable, and more immigrants came from there to here than anywhere else. We all know about Germany and World War 2. I couldn't wait to see the place I was genetically predisposed to hate. I don't like German Shepherds, and all I thought about were those newsreels with those barking canine Nazis. I was a lone voice in my family because, interestingly, I had some family, uncles mostly, who hated Germans(y) and made no efforts to change or make any bones about it. They also displayed their loathing, both nobly and otherwise.

During WW2, I had a number of uncles serving, but 3 really spring to mind as the high and low of the war effort. On the more entrepreneurial / comedic side, one uncle, at 18, was bivouacked on some ice flow in the Aleutians for 3 years with six other guys, with no home leave during that period. They were manning an airstrip. In the first place, my uncle probably would have waited to be drafted, but my grandfather, the cop and sometime trolley car conductor (a totally corrupt cop, and the type of person public transport management would send "praises to heaven" for when he actually returned the trolley, *without trying to sell it*) dragged him down to the recruiting center and made him enlist. No doubt in the hopes he'd be maimed or killed, hopefully both, in no particular order. I wish I was joking about any of this.

But my uncle, always one to see the main chance, clearly understood the business opportunities this unique circumstance presented: an airstrip in the middle of nowhere. He saw the planes fly in and the planes fly out and wondered if he could get his hands on some Scotch type whiskey. Ultimately, this uncle came home with *duffle bags full of money*. He had his stash guarded by a full sergeant while he was conducting business. He was a private but had his uniforms tailor made when he returned to the lower 48. Thereafter, he never worked another day in his life, even when he had to. And he had to. But it never seemed to bother him.

Bravery was not his strong suit, so he inhabits the more comic side of the war. One night, his small group received a radio message that the Japs were landing on this island. They were ordered to go down and defend the beach ... only seven guys. Since my uncle was not going to win the Distinguished Service Cross any time soon, he chose to take his tommy gun and zip himself up in his sleeping bag, saying, "If they want me, they can come and get me." Luckily, it turned out to be nothing, which ultimately helped us win the war. He didn't like Germans and was mystified by me. You'd have loved the guy; everyone did.

Another uncle was a sort of Military Police (MP), but not quite. He guarded prisoners but didn't have the afore-mentioned exalted title. I guess they did some kind of back-ground check on him first and, ultimately, how smart was that? But this uncle began to see the unique opportunities this circumstance presented: namely, the fox guarding the hen-house. Trust me on this. There was no reason, except acute manpower shortages, to put this uncle in the position of upholding the law when his entire life, up to that point, had been dedicated to breaking it. His most minimal transgres-sion was using his rifle to bash in the teeth of the German prisoners he was guarding. He did this routinely as they "tried to escape," as he nonchalantly put it. He used this as an excuse but in reality, who the devil could blame them while being guarded by the Jewish version of Genghis Khan? The prisoner who was still vertical after one of his routine beatings was considered one of the lucky ones. No one ever messed with this uncle, then or after. A tougher SOB rarely walked the earth. He would have easily used his hands, but why bloody them when a nice 10 pound rifle was handy? In and out of prison, he always referred to the "joint" as "college."

My wife asked me one day where this uncle went to school. "My love," I told her, *"you're a long way from Pelican Rapids."* This uncle didn't buy into the whole Master Race thing, either. His war was more of the "personal vendetta" side of the conflict. They obviously had him where they could keep an eye on him, because there was no telling what he could really get into, given the chance.

To make up for these two "heroes," my remaining uncle landed in the First Wave at Omaha Beach and fought all the way thru the Battle of the Bulge. He had a quiet manner, but no one that I ever knew had a bigger spine of steel than this man. He was a dedicated family type, loveable, giving, loyal, and a personal favorite. Also very cute and cuddly … unless you were a Nazi. To you, he gave absolutely no quarter. None. Ever. He told me stories of what could at least be called "revenge killings." And there were a lot of these stories. He killed plenty of the enemy, at every opportunity, and I never heard him once say he regretted any of it. He did his duty and never looked back. This uncle is who won the war for us. Him, and a million others like him.

So, by virtue of having my thoughts influenced by these guys (whom I loved), I wanted to see how much I really hated these people. I was being sort of contrary, as usual, until I got there and realized the food they made was just like my Jewish grandmother's, but not as good. No wonder those reptilian Nazis hated Jews: they were nervous about being usurped, the crumbs. They could masquerade any way they wanted, but the crux of the matter was the contest about who was really the Master Race? Trust me on this: it's the Jews. Have no illusions. Personally, I'm glad of it. We're better off by far.

It took me a couple of visits to my ancestral homeland before I could visit a concentration camp. Up to that point, there wasn't enough alcohol in the world to make me go there, when I could go to a hofbrau and get drunk off my nut for a dollar like every other tourist. Let me see: massive maiming and killing or a brewski it took ten minutes to tap? No contest: it was the Dachau Concentration Camp.

I had to laugh, though. Dachau had a travel brochure that extolled the virtues of this medieval town, which was a wonderful (wunderbar!) place … if you didn't dwell on the death camp's crematorium and gallows. Where's the beer when I need one? Yes, the southern tip of Manhattan is a great place … if you just ignore that gaping hole in the ground. People and the facts don't always mix.

The day I chose to go to Dachau, it was rainy and about 40 degrees. The signs directing me were very unobtrusive, and I could understand that. I wasn't offended; they didn't need neon billboards. The weather conditions should have tipped me off that it wasn't going to be a great day.

I went through the exhibits of casual torture, routine maiming, and the generally convivial atmosphere leading up to this tiny slice of life. Then I crossed the camp and went to the crematorium. Remember I said it was damp and chilly? I came as close to puking my brains out as I have *ever come in my life*. I can still feel my stomach turning over. It smelled, I'm here to tell you, like they stopped burning people yesterday. I was genuinely sick and couldn't really eat for two days. Me! There was a lot of hate in those four ovens.

I won't try to speculate or bore anyone with a "how could this happen?" question. Suffice it to say, it did and could happen, easily, again. People simply hate Jews. I'm sorry, but that's the sad truth. The Skinheads and the stinkin' reptilian Klan are still around, right? Hamas? Oh, I can hear all of us saying we'd stop them before we ever let anything happen. Like we're smarter, more enlightened, and more in tune than people who lived 60 years ago.

Wrong.

I think we're exactly the same and maybe not even quite up to our own previous standards. Our predecessors could tell right from wrong, for example. And they wouldn't bicker about fighting these scum *or* their forebears. Something we all seem to do today, ad nauseum. But we're smarter, remember? Sure we are. Listen, we have to be for the state of Israel; I know that now. Salvation *comes from* the Jews. I finally got a brain in my head. And God himself chose the people, not some knucklehead like me. That should be good enough. "Never again." These words should mean something, more so today than at any other recent time. Go to Dachau, which was small potatoes by their own bloodletting standards, if you need convincing. As if our own 3,000 wasn't enough? The recent perpetrators really wanted the Jews, as they said themselves. And we think they don't *really* exist?

Dateline: Riyadh

But I have to give the devil his due; and he really worked me. I wasn't then politically who I am today. At that time, my experience in the Gulf gave me a perspective, of a sort. In the trenches, where I was, I heard a point of view, especially from the Palestinians, that I wasn't exposed to before and would not be here in America (they had no lobby, then, and really still sort of don't). I always had a thing for the underdog, in this case mistakenly, and they never let me forget it. I was persuaded when I heard their stories (which I heard constantly, like I was some acolyte in a radical mosque), that they had a grudge that was possibly legitimate.

I learned more cultural nuances in the Gulf than I knew existed there. Who knew that the Saudi king decrees whether you are a Saudi or not? You may be from there, but babe, *he* says whether you are Saudi or not. Basically, you're a piece of camel dung or a "real player." And it matters. I had a good friend whose family came to the Kingdom like 4,000 years ago from Iran. He wore the whole get-up and, in my innocence, I thought he was the genuine article. Then I found out the ones who could trace their ancestry back to the original camel thought my friend was a charlatan, a pretender to the throne, a silk hat on a pig. And subtly, they treated him this way. But he still had lots of money. Go figure. Just another one of their routine hypocrisies, I guess.

I'd seen hospitality in Oman from my dear friend, Ali, who makes the usual hospitality look like parsimony (and he remains the sole individual from there who's escaped my wrath). I ate with my right hand and was offered lamb eyes (accept them; you don't have to eat them). I've dined informally with a general (what a party that was! He was the second in command of the Kuwaiti Air Force and loved America. I can only imagine what became of him during DS1) and eaten with the Arab version of a schlepper.

I was treated like gold because I came from a long way away, and I believed in God. This cut a lot of mustard with them until the freakazoids took over and we all had to live in fear. But I discussed their point of view with anyone who'd listen. I thought it needed to be heard, though not necessarily subscribed to. Between two warring sides, there tends to be a middle where the truth resides. This is usually the case, until your "lawyer" blows up 3,000 people, including babies. Then, your case goes right out the window, and you're a no-good bastard. Aren't you?

When 9/11 happened, I saw character flaws in them that I'd taken to be only idiosyncrasies before. After giving it a lot of thought, I'm convinced that their majority's silence is consent. They're actually pleased, secretly, that we got, in their minds, our comeuppance. I saw very few condemnations then from that part of the world, and not many today, either. I know enough about their character and culture that trust becomes a serious issue and skepticism can be an asset for us. I believe, very simply, that most of their hatred is driven by their lack of fortitude. They're severely tempted by the West's open society, and it makes them distraught when they even *get* tempted; then they feel anything but pious. And they hate themselves for their inability to deal with it and their real and perceived marginality.

We, as Christians and Jews, know that temptation and the refusal to give in to it are part of our reason for being here. It builds character and glorifies God. They don't see it as purposeful, and this is crucial to their thinking. Each of these qualities feeds the other, and to compensate, they can turn on a dime, strap on a grenade, and jump on a bus. Or worse, as we have so painfully witnessed. They may think to themselves, maybe if I became a martyr, I could become a really good person in God's eyes. What quicker route to compensate for all one's real or imagined flaws than the way of a martyr? Think about it. It's a very dangerous mindset. And there should be no limits in fighting it. I can't help but think there must be a psychological component to winning this war that we aren't employing, along with the military option. I don't mean "hearts and minds" like Vietnam, but something more subtle. I keep trying to figure out what it is. When I do, I'll call Bush. He needs it. He needs it really badly.

After I moved on from seeing the world on a regular basis (sorry I can't go out with you tonight. I have to be in Saudi Arabia tomorrow ... how cool is that?), I moved back to Philly for a short time.

My Bride, or The Gift That God Gave Me When I Wasn't Looking

But that short time in Philly was long enough to meet my wife. I went out to the pool at my apartment one day and saw this cute little number sitting there whom I'd seen before. (How come nobody else did? 'Cause God put the hex on them.) She laughed at some stupid joke I made and created an opening the width of a hair ... which I proceeded to plow right thru like a freight train.

I was possessed.

I mean, she was cute *and* smart. That's a deadly combination for me. Brunette, short hair, almond shaped eyes, perfect complexion. I was starting a free fall, but I didn't know it yet.

We went to a movie, then went out after, and she told me her life story. What's funny is twofold: first, I'd so little patience in the past hearing this from anyone, and second, how totally out of character this was for my bride. Greater forces were obviously at work.

We went out a couple of times after that. One day we were walking back to the car, it was like a month later, if that, and as she talked, I looked at her. And this was new to me, believe me. I said to myself, Hey, dopey, I think you're falling in love with this girl. Right before this, a screw fell out of my glasses, and she'd had one of those tiny screwdrivers to fix it. No wonder I loved this woman.

But on a serious note, I started thinking about her a heck of a lot. She went on a trip to Fargo to see her family (yes, *that* Fargo) and said to her mom that she may have found "the one." You have no idea how out of character this was, either. My wife would not be that personally revealing about her emotions to anyone. I'd only known her about two months, and she felt this way. Way too impulsive, if you knew her. At about the third month interval I was already totally in love with her while she was, in her mind, still ruminating. I'd enough experience to know that waiting her out was key, and I was right. It was good to be an old grouch, who never hooked up with anyone before. It finally paid off, despite my previous ministrations to God. Then we had *"The Argument."* I called her, and she hung up on me.

I called again, and she hung up again.

OK, life comes down to little moments like this one. I also had the genetic predisposition to never call a woman like this back. Usually, it was one strike and you were out, if that.

Then I called again, and before she could say a word (I was a genius), I told her I was picking her up in front of her building, and she had better be there. She was waiting in her work coveralls at the corner (be still my heart). I was in a gray chalk stripe with matching bowtie and socks (OMG). I was getting bad vibes. I told her we were going to Pat's for a steak. After we drove about a mile, maybe, I said to her that the only way we were going to settle this argument was to get married. She said I was right. Two weeks later, we got married at City Hall in Philly. As of this writing, it's been 17 years of bliss. The easiest thing I've ever done.

The whole experience was the attraction of two equal parts that fit together like cogs in a wheel. We're not really opposites, which you might expect. My wife is from Dent, Minnesota, a town of 165 people (the place is near Pelican Rapids, by the way). I've always joked to her that the population sign is digital, so it can be changed as she comes and goes. Lumpy's (Lisa's) mom's family homesteaded the place a little more than 100 years ago.

Now this is confusing to me personally, though a lot of old immigrants did this very thing: they left the frozen tundra of northern Germany to go to .... the frozen tundra of North America. I'd think they'd be bone tired of freezing their rear ends off and go to Miami or something. Let me understand: you get off the boat in New York and ask which way is Minnesota? You've got to be joking. I wouldn't even do that today. When my people got off the boat from Russia (one step ahead of that dirtbag Czar's Secret Police, who did shoot my grandma's brother, dead, in their living room, for being a Commie), they asked, casually, where the good food was and moved to Philly. Our family's mantra being "Let's Eat," and the apple hasn't fallen far from the tree, which I'm totally down with. It's all about the food, baby.

Being half German and half Irish (though leaning hard to "port" in this case), my bride is not overly emotional and rarely needy. And she's gorgeous. Can you say only a putz wouldn't marry this treasure? And being half Irish, she can drink like a fish and drive home in a straight line. Dang, you couldn't make a woman like this. Even-tempered, smart, beautiful, matched up to an irascible ... (when my family argued, you felt compelled to call 911) and I can't think of anything else positive to say about what I bring to this marriage. I'd love to have that WASPy circumspection as part of my character, but I can't seem to do it. And part of my family is Austrian, the coldest people on earth. My wife actually loves this quality in me, since it's the same intensity that makes me huggy and kissy with the family and spontaneous, like buying them stuff or going to somewhere really good to eat that's unplanned. Li has always told me this is why kids have two parents. I agree, and I'm trying to lose my desire to beat up waiters and airline employees, sort of as an added bonus of my love for her.

This is my honey, with whom I snuggle at every opportunity. Please also note: I am such a girl!

Chapter Six

On the Road Again...

As we got closer to the end of our trip, I'd prepare for the day. I'd pack all the clothes and chattels. Eat breakfast (the usual cholesterol infusion), make a Beanie Baby purchase, and get on the road.

As we flew through Arkansas (not fast enough to suit me), it dawned on me that today was my birthday. I was 50, and I didn't even remember. We don't celebrate our birthdays at home. For the kids, yes, but not us. We don't do the Mother's Day or Father's Day thing, either. We tell each other we love one another almost every day, with feeling. How can you beat that? Despite the events of the last year, my life was perfect in every way. I rarely wavered from this perception, *as it relates to that part*. What's at home is what makes my life, and there were no issues there. I had doubts about myself; some pretty stellar, but I tried to separate this from my wholesome existence I was lucky enough to have.

But I had to ask: where does an Ogre, which I was described as (and a perverted one, too) come from? It doesn't fit. I knew I'd be vindicated one day, since this whole thing was such an outrage to start with. These are two cogs that don't mesh at all, which is why the whole thing was a travesty from Jump Street.

But it was my birthday. Interesting. Was I being reborn, metaphorically speaking, as I came to grips with this painful experience? I hadn't thought of this until now, but I think the theory may have merit. And God could have planned it this way. He wouldn't have made me go thru this meat grinder without a purpose. That intention is what shows me He's there watching me. This vigilance, I believe, being a gift to me.

But 50?

Holy "****." (It's better you don't know this word, but it rhymes with ….) My head was spinning. My kids were playing "Beanie Baby Stag Show," while my own personal Rome was burning.

Holy … est of Holies!

That's past middle age, since I don't subscribe to the massive denial of the general public that seems to think we live to be 100. Thirty-five is middle-aged.

Holy … well …Yikes!

I'm almost dead, chronologically. Physically, I kind of felt like it. My back hurts, my shoulder aches, my stomach has adhesions in the lining, I'm dizzy, I can't see nothin', can't hear squat, my knees make me feel like I'm 80 … with arthritis, and I need constant naps to make up the difference … but thank God I can still drink like a fish and drive home sober!

Happy Birthday to me!

I have imbibed lethal amounts of paint-peeling vodka and not gotten hammered, even on this trip. It must be my Russian ancestry, that magic gene that makes potential drunks sober as priests. I keep experimenting to find that "limit," but so far, no luck. And like a good investigator, I keep trying. In the interests of science, of course.

Good Ol' Texas, We Love You

We'd put on some miles during this trip, literally and figuratively. I examined my whole life and felt pretty damned good about where I'd been and where I got to, emotionally and spiritually. My babies and I hung out for two weeks in a car and rarely, if ever, even bickered. I didn't realize it until after the trip was over and I thought about all we had seen:

famous Civil War Battlefields, our nation's Capitol and all that entails. Gorgeous countryside (I mean, gorgeous), with good food. Good, provocative discussions while eating and otherwise (why was Kennedy actually a very good president and that idiot, Johnson, not?). Saw Grandpa and ate good food again, with him, like six times in two days (as was customary). We stayed in nice places, went in caves, and were loved by the guides. We saw only the good part of Atlantic City, being in the form of that nice guy in the hotel. We met people and scored victories for our country by putting the French in their place (something Bush never did). We actually saw Only, Tennessee, where I said to the gas station lady it sure was beautiful around here in Only. She replied that, yes, Tennessee was beautiful. OK, not exactly what I meant, but how often can you marry your brother and not see any effects?

But more importantly for me at that moment was the personal journey I'd taken. Psychologically, I went from lemons to lemonade. I wasn't quite there yet – this whole thing was traumatic – but inside, I knew the truth would emerge about the incident, as well as me. How could all this self-examination ultimately hurt me? It couldn't, I reasoned. The whole experience would get better as time went by. I didn't *feel* this way, but *knew* this very thing.

And I took my babies with me. As I lay in bed at night, thinking, my mind never really taking a break, I'd feel solace making sure my babes were tucked in; assured they'd bring me breakfast in the morning and the day would be a big one, no matter how insignificant our potential destination. Fortunately, this didn't happen, not even once. My babes got to know me a little. They experienced me with a major problem on my hands, and they were kept isolated from it. Hopefully, they saw the virtue of fortitude. They saw "little Keith," their dad as a kid, driving with me on those same streets where I grew up and saw every detail my failing memory could muster. Hopefully, they saw the virtues of gratitude and loyalty. And they saw a dad who loves them and would do anything for them. Almost anything they asked. And with this, possibly they saw the virtues of love and devotion. And I never let them forget that just because momma wasn't here, we were still the Price family because in essence, she was here. We're never apart. Any of us. Never.

And maybe, just maybe, they'd undertaken a journey, too. Someday they may find it in their hearts to tell me, and we can gratefully relive the whole thing again.

But here we were after our journey that, I guess, had to end at some point. As we approached home, it was raining. When we got closer to the house, the weather cleared, and the sun hung there like a golden guinea pasted in the sky (my old college professor used to greet us with this phrase). Another rebirth, I guess, of a sort.

Lisa came out to greet us with a big smile on that beautiful face. The kids were excited to see her, no less than I. They ran to her.

We were finally home, in every sense of the word. A place of solace and succor. A place of warmth and familiarity. A place we loved. At last.

Tara.

Epilogue

You know those folks who get shot out of a cannon at the circus? They load you in (and you do this voluntarily, I might add), they arrange the explosives, set off the charge, and out you go, flying through the ether, unsure if you'll actually hit that net they set up for you. But you usually do. You hit, bounce around a lot, settle down from the incipient nausea (if it's me doing this), and you climb down, somewhat acrobatically and settle onto solid ground. You're different somehow from when you were launched at the start. How could you not be? If you're an amateur cannon-cocker like I am, you don't do this too often, if ever. But sometimes, it happens to you symbolically.

It happened to me. I got blasted out and landed on my feet. I could've lived without the parabola through the air, but you have to make the net somehow. And I did.

As I write this, I'm in a cast almost up to my shoulder, from the middle of my palm. I'm the one-handed, yet deadly, typist. I'd have finished this manuscript a long time ago if I wasn't "Mr. One Finger." I guess I could do worse, since it isn't *that* finger.

Distance gives perspective, whether it be time or space. Like the injury I suffered riding my bike, it will heal. The bone was broken, it was set, and it healed but left a scar. This pretty much says it all. Any injury will heal, emotional or physical. I've now suffered both and survived more or less intact. I feel almost perfect, in every sense. I'm grateful.

A war is waging in Iraq, as I write this epilogue. There's an irony to this, actually. I've been writing about the Gulf, and here we are, up to our eyeballs in that … place. I haven't lost sight of the fact that we have to prevail; that we're fighting an offensive war, which is how it should be. I have little regard for any part of that area anymore or, I regret to say, the people in it, for the reasons I explained in the foregoing chapters. I care only about us and our allies; no one else. If they turned most of the Middle East into a parking lot tomorrow (which we won't), I don't know if I'd really care, and that's very sad to me, given the good times I managed to experience despite all their efforts to take the fun out of absolutely everything (in deference to their culture, not necessarily their religion, as they mistakenly preach). I have a sneaking suspicion most of the people living there wouldn't care much either. Life isn't that important, including their own, and this is the most tragic aspect of the whole thing; this gift from God thought of so cavalierly. Who'd believe an attitude such as this? So I just hope we fight to win, at our government's upper levels.

Or get out, threatening Armageddon the next time. This strategy would make even the most intransigent person understand, even our enemies, who I've come to know so intimately and so well. This is the only temporal solution; the only one. It's come too far for the healing power of Christian love to make a difference. Individually yes, but we're talking millions here. History makes me think a lot of these people are unapproachable and truly dedicated to our demise. Remember I mentioned their guilt? It can be a deadly motivator, with the West as the potential victims and whom they see as the source of all their troubles, exemplified particularly by the USA. And so we fight and pray for understanding. I must leave the real solutions to God and God alone. Or go out of my mind. But I want to end this on a happy note, since the rest is beyond our individual control.

At home, more immediately, the kids are fine. We're looking at colleges with the oldest, which freaks me out. The youngest is working and earning money, his God. Lisa is still the same, beautiful and good. I look around, and I'm extremely happy. I made the journey to "Everest" and lived to tell. I have given up my anger (don't fall over dead) and feel much better for it. It created a membrane over my life that affected me as an employee, a husband, and a father. May I say, now and forever, the hell with that ever happening again?

So, my life is the usual routine. Right now the kids are driving me crazy so that I take them to the mall, in order for them to eat sugar for three hours. Lisa is cleaning (my house should be the poster child for *Immaculate Living* magazine). It feels like that time of the day where I will be compelled to take a nap (ah, bliss!). I'll go upstairs, perhaps fold a little laundry (such a good husband) before I lie on the bed and tell myself how lucky I am, before I fall asleep. I may not recite those exact words but will settle down into the feeling and let it … envelope me. I always seem to do this. Recall, if you will, the constant thinking about my exact place in this universe. No turning off this brain, with anything short of a lobotomy, done with a Gamma Knife.

Sometimes, not every time, but a lot of the time, without sounding like some deranged, sandal-wearing, cave-dwelling acolyte, I feel inside how much I love God, despite my personal travails and life's travails in general, from which everyone suffers; some pretty profoundly and more than I suffer. I really think about this love because … it comforts me. With everything good I've said on these pages, how can I not acknowledge this as a routine fact of my existence? That it's something, a good thing, which lies just below the surface; and so accessible to me. He has blessed me and loves me. Assured my loved ones and I are being looked after, I fall asleep peacefully. This is my way of counting sheep, and it rarely fails me.

At some point during my nap, Lisa will start vacuuming 6 inches from my head, or the kids come in like a herd of elephants to use the computer, rousting me ever so ... un-gently. The Blitzkrieg across France was quieter (after all, how much noise does an immediate surrender actually make?). I'm sorry, I can't help myself from taking this parting shot at France or Nazis, Turtles or Nazis, Amway people, or Nazis, desert people or Nazis or that reptile who almost ruined my special moment with England's own, Miss Gorgeous. And did I mention Nazis?

It's been fun. And I hope you had a good time joining me and letting you laugh at me voluminously. I actually really enjoy that part. Despite the appearance, I can't take myself too seriously, and I hope you won't take me that way either. You know by now when I mean it, creature of extremes that I am.

I wouldn't have wanted anyone else to come along for the ride. I wouldn't trade any of you, or any of this, for all the riches in the world. Because I already possess them, don't I?

God bless you ... and He will. Just *ask*. I mean, look at me!

Keith Price
Dallas, TX.
February, 07

P.S. It's 5 o'clock somewhere...!

Endnotes

ⁱ I was on a trip to DC when I was in high school. As part of the bus tour, in order to prevent total boredom, the guide asked trivia questions. He asked, "Who said, 'Damn the torpedoes, full speed ahead!' "

This was at the height of Watergate, so I answered, "Richard Nixon!"

ⁱⁱ I'm no art critic or even that knowledgeable, but I think that one essential element of real art shows the influence of previous work, like Picasso was influenced mainly by Cezanne.

I'm not sure how poo and artistic impulse are irresistibly drawn together unless you lack talent. Surprisingly, it appears obsession with one's own putrid bodily emanations has become a popular art form, funded by an insane government. Personally, I think these fixations are worthy only of study by qualified physicians.

ⁱⁱⁱ Like going to Mecca, you have to go there at least once before you pass on, because I'm not sure they have steak *where I'm going*, and it's more likely to be well done.

ⁱᵛ I'm sure some of you have seen the movie *Sideways*. It mostly deals with wine appreciation – and I fully appreciate it, by the way – but with all the great wine in that movie, all I could think about was the food in those California restaurants. Even in fine ones, and I have been in several, the food simply ... stinks. Except at Thomas Keller's place.

ᵛ With all the free mentions of food and restaurants in this seminal work, there had better be a BIG payoff for yours truly.

ᵛⁱ I'm writing this well after the fact, but I still feel its mark on me, which tells you many things, I would guess. It isn't a cataclysm, mind you, but a life-altering event somewhere in the past. I often ask myself, why did I have to go through this? Then someone mentioned that the other person may have been the one that had to go through it, and I was merely scenery. Whoa.

ᵛⁱⁱ A Black and Tan is a fermented beverage of the ale variety. Yum.

ᵛⁱⁱⁱ And I saw a psychiatrist three times that went on record in this matter that I was perfectly normal, proving what I already knew: she was examining the wrong person. I also had very colorfully stuck up for some people against an arbitrary-type imbecile, and that didn't help. I wasn't myself, since I didn't usually act this way. But I felt compelled to stick up for subordinates, which I thought was my moral responsibility.

ⁱˣ When we visit my bride's hometown of 150 people, she claims I need at least 20 mg of valium just to survive it, taken 4 times per day. This isn't true. I actually kind of like it. I just couldn't live there.

ˣ There was an Indian Camp set up to give the tourists, i.e. the Price Family Robinson, a feel for the past in this place. It didn't work; it seemed contrived. It wasn't natural, if you will, like that freakin' bridge, WHICH WE LOVED!

ˣⁱ Recent work I've read determined that Hitler was such an anti social strootz that he was compelled to do these horrible things; destined in his own mind, to do them, before he even did them. For example, sign a treaty and attack Poland, sign a treaty and attack Russia. Each time he escalated the stakes, but he'd determined his course of action from when he was schlepping paintings around Vienna. Churchill clearly saw this, and Chamberlain did not.

ˣⁱⁱ As I said, I never engaged a professional woman. There was a period in my life that lasted longer than I hoped it would where I actually thought that sex was love, so I craved it. It never dawned on me that the only time I really enjoyed it was when there actually was some modicum of love involved (I never had real love until I met my wife). I forced myself into situations that were wholly empty on every level, and I was left feeling miserable.

But the craving put me in some insane situations, not the least of which was thinking I could mechanically go thru the motions and like it. When I was in Amsterdam I went to the Red Light District actually thinking I would make it with a "pro." I'd been in Saudi for 3 weeks and Lord knows. When I turned the corner to the place, all I saw were half-naked chicks, sitting on bar chairs behind plate glass windows, reading the newspaper. Hubba hubba. And 300 shrimpy Middle Eastern types walking around with their pants around their ankles.

Can you say party or what?

I ended up in my hotel room, lamenting what my life had come to. What was I thinking?

The other time I was standing outside the Clift Hotel in San Francisco, holding a tube of toothpaste I had just bought. A car pulled right in front of me with 3 women inside and scared the beejeebees out of me. They asked if I wanted to party. Then they said (I'm not making this up), that they didn't mean to scare me. They knew they had, because I'd squeezed the toothpaste out of the tube and onto my hand. Popped the top right off the thing. This is the sum total of my experiences with working women. Somewhere they're still laughing.

Metaphorically, the toothpaste fulfilled my "professional woman" requirement. I mean, how perfect was that? God is still laughing about this episode; I know I would be.

xiii When I made that trip, I stayed at a different B and B. It marked one of the only times, in all my travels that I encountered someone who appeared to truly hate Americans. This woman couldn't stop saying rude and cutting things … and we were her customers. We actually paid for the room and left without spending the night, because I didn't want to give this nut job any more ammunition. I was appalled by her behavior, and though I was a pacifist in those days, I desperately wanted to punch her in her limey mouth, God forgive me. I should have offered to fund her in a weight loss program, which she would have really hated, if you get my drift.

xiv I read some recent material that tried to explain French arrogance. What was said was they hated to ask, and then got angry when you actually helped them. Good luck working with that point of view. If I wanted to be around attitudes like that, I'd be around my kids more …

xv My school was quite a place. Academically, I never connected to it (or any other place until St. Joe). The teachers were not nurturers, and they simply hated me. Unusual choice of profession for a person allegedly dedicated to shaping young minds. If they really didn't dislike me intensely, they gave one heck of an imitation. To the brilliant students (one with brilliantined hair and running to fat, and another I can only pray for his sake is out of the closet now) they couldn't do enough. Any mook could do that. Had you seen these ladies, you'd understand God's sense of humor. Put it this way — well, I can't put it that way. For the one teacher who paid attention to me, I was his number one student, against all comers, and on a test(s) got a better grade than all of the geniuses. I looked over at one genius to see the look on his face: I actually recall doing it because I knew it was a lock. He was the type that routinely wore one of those bright orange hunting hats with the furry earflaps because his mother made him, with no thought to the ridicule it would elicit, especially by me. I like to think that he also knew Dr. Freud personally.

xvi I told the Tea Shop owner I wanted to buy ... his life, and change places with him. How did I see the countryside there? I rode around with the postman in his Royal Mail truck for 4 hours and stopped for tea. It cost $2.00. He had those gigantic, Dickensonian keys attached to his belt to open some really old locks.

xvii I met these adorable septuagenarians from Peebleshire; she was 90, and he was 87. I partied with them, so to speak. They told me they knew Robert Burns personally, they were that old.

Printed in the United States
107224LV00008B/1-6/P

"THE ODYSSEY AND THE IDIOT"

A Road Trip Through America ... With My Kids!!

By

Keith J. Price

First published by Dog Ear Publishing
4010 W. 86th Street, Ste H
Indianapolis, IN 46268
www.dogearpublishing.net

dog ear
PUBLISHING

ISBN: 978-159858-517-9
This book is printed on acid-free paper.

Printed in the United States of America

For JEG, for R, for SF, for WFR

And mostly for my dad, who passed during the writing of this book.

Dad, just this simple sentiment for you: you were a terrific guy, and I truly miss you.

For Lumpy, and for the BooBoos.

Last, but not least: for all those I love, and who know it.

There is a passage in Matthew and probably in the other Gospels, too (and I am paraphrasing) where the disciples are in a small boat with Jesus. A violent storm begins, and the disciples panic while Jesus sleeps serenely. They are in fear for their lives, they wake Him, and He reprimands them for having so little faith.

Spiritually speaking, I think we've all been in that boat.

I was standing in a Christian bookstore and saw a painting representing this Gospel story. I had labored previously to find an epigram that would encapsulate my book. I needed to look no further. Not only that, He found me, as usual.

TABLE OF CONTENTS

Preface

You picked up this book and, for that simple act, I want to thank you. Possibly it was the cover that drew you to it. I envision the cover as a picture of my face with my hands over my ears and my wide mouth screaming, while my kids hover "innocently" in the background. This is kinda how I picture my life. Or, maybe you were attracted to the title, which implies that a journey of some sort was undertaken — it was — and an idiot (yours truly, though a very lucky idiot) was able to tag along and reap the thoroughly unexpected benefits. Once again, the divine plan was smarter than this author. And I'm no longer surprised by it.

Though at first I wouldn't admit it, I am someone who's been blessed beyond reason. What did I ever do to be showered with such good fortune? I've often asked myself this question, which has been a constant refrain in my life. Maybe I'm just now finding the answer and just now being comfortable with it.

If by reading just the preface you laugh or you're compelled to think about your own kids; or if, after reading the book, you see a unique perspective on things or related to something you didn't already know (which is very difficult these days with TV sadly taking away all of life's mysteries), then I have *far exceeded* even my wildest dreams. And for this, I am grateful. It was my goal.

It's no easy task to influence anyone's thinking. This was a difficult lesson for me to learn and *it took years*. I may have actually accidentally changed someone's mind years ago, in my youth, and subsequently thought it was the norm rather than the exception. Not a great jumping off point, if you want peace in your life. Though I can't say the road wasn't rocky, I learned this valuable lesson and am somehow better for it. Life has a way of teaching you things, even if you are a reluctant pupil.

It's taken five decades to write this book. Not the actual writing of it; that took about 2 years. I had to *live* the 50 years, in order to have something I considered worthy of sharing. In this respect, and in many others, I'm an elitist: if it isn't awesome, it's tiresome. I'd tried several times, to be sure, to write something of interest, and I'd always found the results either lacked profundity (usually) or were not remotely funny (often). And I threw them away.

Note: I was always told never to do this. And those folks who told me this may have been right ... if I was Ernest Hemingway. I'm not Ernest Hemingway, though I do have half a beard and that is as close as I could come to him, as far as having anything in common.

I simply needed to live a life and make careful mental notes about the experience. My desire to "create" was not in proportion to anything noteworthy I had to say. Maybe finding this equilibrium is what it means to be a writer. This book took *work*. Getting it to where I wanted it, like the perfectionist I am, didn't help streamline matters. It was like giving birth ... but without the fun of the sedatives. I've heard people call art a labor of love. Labor? That I'll give you. Love? I'm too young to know that answer yet, and I'm 50 already.

And, like labor, or so I'm told, when it's over, you have no problem once the baby comes in doing it all over again. There's a life lesson in there somewhere. I've always enjoyed looking deeply into life's truths and mysteries; sometimes believing that some great thinker had to contemplate these realities first in order to intelligently access them. And despite this predisposition of mine, sometimes the answer can be very simple. If nothing else comes out of all my experience, that much I do know. And that may be something worth passing on.

Chapter One

The Adventure Begins:
a Sometimes Historical and Sometimes
Hysterical Journey to Find God.

And, Myself.

With my kids (13 and 10 when the adventure began), it's been non-stop hysteria. To be clear, it's the laughing-type hysteria they create. I supply, at other times, the more loathsome variety, which I'm very sorry to have to tell you. But with my babies (and despite me), between tanning their hides and pummeling good manners into them, it's been more rewarding and enjoyable than I ever thought possible, *i.e., like for the first 33 years of my life...*

I'd never even *entertained* the possibility I'd ever want kids. Kids? You've got to be kidding. I mean, think about it: I could wind up with a kid like me!

God forbid.

And God, God love Him, gave me two ... exactly like me! He may have thought He was punishing me, or so I thought originally. But I subsequently discovered that He'd given me a gift of considerable proportions. He's much smarter than I. This is why He is God, and by trying to out-think him I am, well, idiotic springs to mind. What was I thinking?

Lesson #1 in Life

Never try to outthink God or His intentions.

or:

... you'll end up naked under fluorescent lights,

... with mirrors everywhere,

... while images of your lumpy nakedness are beamed to an unsuspecting public,

... and, as a final insult, your cellulite is magnified in a pop-up box. Lucky you.

Lesson #2 in Life (and this is important)

Never forget Lesson #1.

So, here's a look at things from the perspective of a 49-year-old, middle-aged, white boy, at the time of this experience:

One day I was minding my own business when God, in His infinite wisdom, gave me a chance to take an unplanned "vacation," the length of which was up to me. However, "they" clearly expressed "they" didn't want me around for at least six weeks. They didn't use those exact words, but the subtext was pretty darn clear, even to a dimwit like I am.

How many middle-aged executives of fairly prosperous means get a chance to take time off and be truly away from the office? I mean:

> … no phones,
> … no calls,
> … no email,
> … no faxes (remember those?),
> … no meetings, and no planning for them,
> … no conferences,
> … no dispute resolutions,
> … no interactions with corporate,
> … no request forms for paper clips,
> … no stupid questions, with obvious answers,
> … no padding one's expense account,
> … no long walks from the garage to the office (the Bataan Death March was shorter),

No *nothing.*

Just *off.*

It was something to treasure. Surely, it would be for me. I could hardly wait.

And I hated every minute of it...

Hard to believe when you wish for something like this periodically for most of your business career and suddenly, it happens to you. I'd frequently wished for time away where I knew money was still coming in strong and I could relax. Who wouldn't? Yes, I'd wished for this many times during periods of particular stress (though perspective has showed me those periods were more blissful than stressful, comparatively speaking). I'd guess most business people my age would like this to happen, under optimal conditions. OK, so there's the rub. The conditions were not optimal; they weren't even in the same *hemisphere* as optimal.

When I was in college I majored in literature, with a particular interest in Shakespeare. I was old enough then (a hundred years ago) to understand most of what the playwright was trying to express. (And whoever did it better, really?). Mostly, Shakespeare wrote in five acts, with the critical action, particularly in the Tragedies, happening in the third act, like scene two or three. It's not exactly a mathematical formula, but a pattern Shakespeare pretty much adhered to.

If I broke my life into acts, like on a continuum, and if I assumed that a person lived to be 100, the crucial, life-altering experiences would happen at around, say, age 50 ...

Shakespeare, that Scram and "Ham-let" eatin' British clairvoyant

All I can say is, he was smarter than even I thought. Though I'm sure Shakespeare never planned to be looked at in quite this way (I don't think), my life-altering experience occurred on my theoretical continuum like a shot fired from a rifle directly into the bull's eye.

And right into my heart.

No, my wife didn't fall in love with another guy or get cancer. My babies didn't die in car accidents nor have their bodies crippled by some unpredictable evil force. The people I truly love were (and are) still safe and warm.

No, for me it was a little different. Vile, self-serving accusations were made against my character. It sounds so trivial when I write it down like this. And it usually is trivial … when it happens to someone else. For an individual for whom character is everything, the accusations left my integrity, in my view, shredded. I would never have believed the issue's magnitude had it not befallen me. But something good, even initially, came out of it: I better understood people's anguish … when it was *credible*, now that I had, in the past, seen when it clearly wasn't. That experience could become a commendable attribute for anyone "down the road." That's a good place be, "down the road," if you don't have to make the journey to get there first.

My efforts since this happened have been to re-assemble the truth, both of the event and of myself, clearly the more important truth. And I'll never be the same again. I believe this. Many people had incorrect perceptions about the accusations, and I was powerless to do a darn thing about it. Trust me, not easy for a take-charge guy like myself.

In the parallel universe that I unknowingly inhabit, the accusation *is everything,* regardless of the truthfulness of it. Pretty dang gut-wrenching, I'm telling you. Sitting there, being assaulted, and having to take it, because the space between just enough protesting and too much protesting …

well, you couldn't slip Paris Hilton's IQ thru it. I wish I had enough arrogance or selfishness to not give a damn, like Rhett Butler. Alas, I didn't, and I still don't. But I know people that do, and sometimes I envy them ... until I come to my senses.

Sexual innuendo was my crime; the accusation of an employee. It sounds like I'm making it up, but I'm not. It seems so downright stupid, but after I was accused, I was treated as if I had a highly contagious form of leprosy, or I'd become a personal neutron bomb: when I came around, all life vanished.

But there it is. It seems so small; a half-baked version of sexual harassment is the best I can figure. Because I'd never heard the term spoken before in the company of anyone with a still-functioning brain stem, I never learned what it meant. But I learned quickly that it was powerful enough to get me thrown out and delivered, with malice aforethought, into a spiraling, nausea-inducing tailspin. And here I sit today. I'm over the nausea, I'm happy to say, but the whirlwind the whole episode created still shakes me up from time to time. Especially when it rears its ugly trailer park head.

So where did the happy part of all of this come from? The happy part that made me want to write this book? I was sitting on the sofa (something I do extraordinarily well), with nothing but time on my hands. Clearly, I needed to do something. It's not in my nature to sit around and ruminate (sit around, no; ruminate, yes). But what could I do? I started thinking ... clean the garage? No. Trim the trees out back? No. Spackle the walls where they were cracked? No, primarily since I have no idea *how to* spackle. Torture the kids? Enticing, but no. Then, it slowly came to me ...

The kids were off. *I was certainly off*, the irony of which was not lost on me.

A family road trip!

What a great idea, I said to myself. After all, nothing says "road trip" like profound mental anguish. Keith J. Price, come on down! This is just what the doctor ordered. So what if my brain chemistry was all twisted up from stress? Brain chemistry be damned! Gee, I was starting to sound like a real manly man for once and possibly even starting to act like one. I hardly recognized myself.

Great. I believe it would start to set things right. I envisioned the beauty of the Tennessee countryside, the lush back roads of old Virginny (with colonnades by the porch), the Shenandoah Valley, the majesty of our nation's capitol, and the rolling farmlands of Pennsylvania. So what if we had to go through east Texas and Arkansas to get there first? We'd just do that part *really, really fast*.

We'd drive up to New Jersey from Texas (OK, so I haven't seen less appealing bookends since Clinton and Lewinsky). We'd see all that we could. We'd educate ourselves. I could be "dad," imparting my awesome wisdom, in the hopes that my babies would listen to it for the first time. How many chances would I get to do something like this again?

This wasn't to "bond," since we'd done that since the babies were born. There was something more to be had here, the chance for me to make a personal journey; one on so many different levels. To let time and space work their magic for me. I could get away. I could think about myself and where I was now and would be in the future. I'd be with my family, individuals more important to me than my own life. And I could listen for their observations of the setting, the history, the whatever, that they were so capable of making. And most importantly, I'd listen to their observations related to me. Especially from my babies who, for some reason, always cut to the truth.

And this is where the hysterically funny adventure begins: Price Family Robinson ... but without the loincloths.

Since the climax of my life's play had already taken place (and please, Lord, no more knives in the eye), this road trip would occur at about the time when I would find myself if I appeared at Stratford or Broadway. We'd reached the crescendo of the play, but the players remained on this side of the river.

Like Robert Burns said, "the best-laid plans of mice and men, often go astray." He wrote in dialect, and for our purposes, I'm writing in a form of English we can understand. If I didn't, it would look something like this: "Ah, the best Laid schemes o' myce and men gone oft aglay." You can see the need to paraphrase. Of course, what he meant (and he's one of my favorite poets of all time) was that no matter what we mere mortals do, there is the possibility of cruel fate taking its turn.

Though not cruel in the worst sense, my wife Lisa Marie Price nee Clark of Dent, Minnesota, couldn't make the trip with us. (And yes, Virginia, there is a Dent, Minnesota; it's near Pelican Rapids). A setback of sorts, because none of us had ever been apart from each other for more than 15 minutes, unless we had to be at work or doing something equally tedious. It bothered me to go without her, but I thought some semblance of my plan could still be met. My wife and I are so totally a couple that no unsolicited emotions (like jealousy or anger for being apart from us) could contaminate the mix. She agreed the greater good of the goal should still be met and damn the torpedoes.[i]

My wife packed for us. My bride, it should be known right now, is unrivaled in the art of packing and anticipation. Need a Kleenex® while visiting some cavern in Nowheresville, Tennessee? Check that jacket pocket (which she just knew you'd be wearing that day). Need to get rid of it? Check the other pocket. There, dollars to donuts, is a GLAD® bag labeled "dirty tissues + any other kid-generated detritus." The woman is uncanny, I'm telling you.

But she can be a little extreme in her motherliness, too. I have no problem with it, but our kids frown a little about it. The babes won't go to the movies with her. Period. She sneaks in (you can't make this up) healthy snacks: carrots, Goldfish® crackers, bottled water. Forget, for the moment, the sheer embarrassment to me of sneaking food into a movie theater, something I could never bring myself to do. But genetic make-up clearly takes precedence here, and I'll never understand it; the healthy well-being of the children is *every-thing* ... and damn the torpedoes! Besides, who wouldn't jump at the chance to watch *The Lord of the Rings 2* while munching on organic rice cakes? Let me see ... if I confine my thinking to North America only? 240 million people.

When they go with dad, it's all the junk they can eat, so their cell phones are programmed to defibrillate them at a moment's notice as they empty the snack bar. But all my arguments aside, I'm sorry, kids. She wins. There's no other way, and please trust me on this. Someday you'll understand. *She wins.*

I've learned as a parent that no matter what we try to program into our kids, it seems to end up, at best, a crap shoot. That's as of today (though my optimism tells me this will end up untrue). It can be discouraging as we continually expend emotional energy and create psychological stratagems to positively modify their behavior and influence their thinking (brainwashing by the Commies took less effort).

I have this vision running thru my head all the time: they'll be out with their friends one day, after drinking enough booze to poison Waterloo, Iowa, looking for the magical hangover cure that every college kid seeks like Crusaders sought the Holy Grail (it's Mexican food, by the way). And they'll be eating boiled-to-death Wheatena and strawberries, followed up with de-flavorized, non-fat / non-sugar, fruit yogurt. Thanks to their parents.

Can you say party, or what? What not just rear them in a Skinner box?!

Eating the containers would be more beneficial nutritionally. And all because of their psychologically unbalanced parents, so obsessed with their bodily well-being, we should:

... be living in an ashram,

... eating curried, macrobiotic locusts,

... while monotonously reciting passages from the Bhagavad Gita, like some deranged Hindu Pod People.

I just get goose flesh knowing they will have us to thank one day for having them roundly ostracized by those other semi-normal teenage burnouts as "those Price kids, the ones from another planet" (where they always recycle and sing "We Are the World"). I am, I admit, a knowing accessory, after the fact. This will be one of my lovingly enduring legacies to my kids.

And this will be my wife's legacy: the "Angel of Death" to movie snackers everywhere.

Lesson #3 in Life

Let them eat McDonald's.

They will anyway. Any efforts to the contrary will be futile. But don't let mom catch you, honies.

So, we prepped. Actually, Lisa prepped, we waited. We all said a tearful goodbye and set off to wherever the fates and careful planning decreed. We started driving northeast; the kids firmly planted in the back, with me and the cookies / other goodies in the front (some of which were "healthy" and to be avoided at all costs, or eaten if we somehow made it to the base camp of Everest on this trip).

We drove. The sun was up, big, salmon-colored, and inviting, and we had so much to see, experience, and maybe to grow from. And we were heading toward it.

Chapter Two

The Road to Memphis,
or "Look Out, Elvis,
Here Come the Prices!"

Early am

The weather was good. Clear and slightly hot. This is the Texas of three seasons I have come to love: it was hot, it is hot, and it will be hot. I put gas in the Avalanche (the worst designed, yet coolest, car ever). Lucky for me, my wife, "Miss Detail," asked the kids to keep track of every expense we incurred, so she'd have an idea of how much we spent. This is how she secretly got back at me for not coming with us: give the kids a task whose primary goal is to destroy their dad while driving him crazy … at the same time, if possible. This is something they will always rise to. Lisa asked that the kids do this – keeping the expense part, though not for some skinflint reason. The driving me crazy / destruction was an added bonus.

My bride keeps the books, and this is the way she wants it. This is a hill I chose not to die on long ago. She wishes it this way. I could care less, personally. Here's my thought process: amount in account (a guess) minus how much we spent recently (a guess) plus how much we have stashed but not detailed (a guess) equals I am content. Besides, I asked her to keep the books because I hate doing it. I mean, I haven't written a check in 18 years, and if I did, it would be on the "Antiques Roadshow" as an antique itself. We do it her way. If this sounds "whipped" as we go on, listen and learn. Indulge me. This will pay off for you. Trust me.

Lesson #4 in Life

Learn to say 'meeeeeoooowwww'!

I finished filling the gas tank and handed over the receipt to the CFO of this trip, our son, Alexander. I couldn't help but really notice the prices, which were not cheap. This was before September 11 and since I'd heard the drumbeat of the first Gulf War being one for oil, I couldn't help but think what morons were perpetrating this hoax. If the war were for oil, we'd have so much supply gas stations would *pay us* for filling the tank. I mean, seriously. We'd be lighting cigarettes with gas and maybe even giving some away for free to the French.

The babes were quiet. It was pretty early, and they were absorbed in what they were doing (which excluded poking each other with ice picks, at this point, but the day was still young). Unlike other families, we don't have a DVD player for trips. It was a gamble, but we made several road trips of 13+ hours, and the kids seemed to manage all right. After all, when my wife and I were young, we traveled substantial distances with just an AM radio.

In my case, I also had two sisters who were hell-bent on seeing me punished at every opportunity just because I was still breathing, which they saw as a continuing insult to their well-being. I have to give them credit though, as I look back. They *always* managed to get me blamed for everything. When our father used to freak on me, my sisters quietly laughed until their heads were about to explode. My sisters had real talent for this, and the Mafia never set up people as good as they did.

As we headed out, I had nothing directly on my mind, But I began thinking about various things, such as the lush scenery. (According to my bride, who knows me, I never stop thinking.) I noticed that the scenery got lusher as we traveled east from Dallas. Prettier. The flora wasn't the kind we would see later in the eastern part of the US, where the flora can have color and lushness because the sun doesn't reduce everything to a cinder like it does in Texas. The flora that can survive east of Dallas, are thicker than pretty much anywhere else in the state . After a night of several martinis, they could even be considered beautiful. I mean *several martinis.*

Meanwhile, the hypnosis of the road tuned out a lot of distractions. Though my head never stopped working, as I said, I began to experience a kind of "free association." This free association happens each morning when I lie in bed, too. I consistently try to get ahold of time and squarely place myself somewhere in it. I do this constantly; I try to determine, within the course of my life, my exact position. Does this make sense? It isn't about financial goals or what I own. I endeavor to gauge exactly where I am emotionally or psychologically and sometimes spiritually, whenever I have a chance to rest my head from the more immediate needs I always seem to have. This mental exercise gives me perspective. It's a big reality out there, right? And a sand fly like myself needs to know his place in this cosmos, or I won't be able to navigate through my own chaotic existence. Maybe it's a control thing; I don't know. I do know I feel more secure when I take advantage of these occasional opportunities. It's almost a prayerful state, and I welcome it. Basically, I ask myself what about me needs to improve. Yes, I really ask this, and not as a self-indulgence. The Jesuits pounded this simple motif into my head years ago, and it's a creed that serves me well. Usually.

I find the theme of some, if not most, of these daydreams to be of a more spiritual nature. It isn't always about

God, as I said. But I do drift through the past and try to determine His thoughts on my behavior as I experienced, for
example, love (or what I thought was love), compassion,
anger (sometimes righteous, mostly not), sex, indifference,
manipulation. I always think I ultimately did right, in the face
of all these. Not necessarily nicely or delicately, in any of
them, even when it was called for, but right. My impulse was
always to do so, though I'm here to tell you, *in writing*, I
didn't always. And I regret it. Following the moral compass
that is my core wasn't always easy. It just wasn't. And most
recently, I still did right. I worked this over in my head
enough times to know. Total, detailed perspective would help
me. This was as clear as it had ever been. This time however,
it wasn't a choice, like it usually was, if I wanted to survive
the recent past.

After about an hour in the car, the babes started to come
alive. Visions of Cracker Barrel began dancing in their heads.
By the way, these Cracker Barrel people are downright home-
grown geniuses. Besides having good, acceptable food – to a
critic like I am, no small feat – they have their locations at
exactly the right spot on every highway. It's uncanny, really.
Exactly 2.5 hours after you leave Dallas, there's a big ol'
Cracker Barrel in Tyler, "jest a settin' thar waitin' " when it's
time for breakfast. The Cracker Barrel folks also have the
most gorgeous buying office I've ever worked in: a mountain
hunting lodge with all the knickknacks in it. I love these people. And we never miss a meal there when we travel to
Florida, to a place called "Redneckville," where we go every
single year.

And my son never misses a single billboard advertising
the locations, even while sleeping: "IT IS 7.3 MILES TO
EXIT 65, MAKE A LEFT, THERE'S CRACKER

BARREL!" (With all this advertising, if this book gets published I'd better be eating for free for a very long time.)

My son, God love all 40 inches of him, is *the worst* backseat driver you could ever imagine. I'm going to start leasing him out to people I hate. He can torture you, in his quest for knowledge.

"Who honked?"

"Why did they honk?"

"What did *you do*, dad?"

"Doesn't he know the left lane is for passing?"

"How frustrating … God!"

All this while he listens to Green Day for the 100th time since 7 am.

I think Cracker Barrel has this all figured out. Because just when I'm ready to murder my kid and bury his ornery remains … it's Beanie Baby Time! Damn the torpedoes!

But first, we eat … like we're going to the electric chair. The kids have become models of efficiency (which, believe it or not, is actually more my trait than Miss Kleenex®'s, Lisa). It goes like this: (1) read menu; (2) give dad specific instructions (and God forbid I make mistake); (3) double-check orders (them); (4) run to gift shop. All in less than 5 minutes. I feel like that guy in the *The Longest Day* taking that bridge from the hairy Germans: "All in less than 15 minutes. But we can expect a counter attack soon," he said. How true. But let me go on the record, Major Howard. I'd rather fight the no-good Germans with a piece of wilted alfalfa than bring my kids pancakes with the wrong topping. I'm joking, of course. But I'd rather, as a general rule of thumb, kill Nazis than order breakfast for my kids. At least one of these exercises would be appropriately rewarded.

Lesson #5 in Life

Nazis bad, pancakes good.

"Attack of the Beanie Babies" or "Where's My Swiss Bank Account When I Need It?"

About ten years ago, maybe more, I was waiting in an airport God knows where, and I saw these cute little animal things. I bought two. How could I have guessed that what started as a sweet, endearing, little stuffed toy would:

a) make otherwise idiot people into newly obsessed idiot people. And create a book for how to retail and collect Beanie Babies, for ^%#*'s sake. A best seller! The whole process mystifies me, but here I sit, toiling away, while the idiot people relax on a beach in Hawaii collecting interest like some podunk lottery winner ... as they lay right next to those Amway Ponzi schemers.

b) become the bane of my existence.

So there we were at the Cracker Barrel in Tyler, Texas. The babes made their way back to the table after making their foray into the "Land of Beanie." OK, so "short stuff" may be a little old for this. OK, so "big stuff" may be a little old for this, too. But they are in possession of some higher moral calling, apparently. I know it involves me and torture. I'm still trying to figure it out.

Besides, we're on vacation! And nothing says "vacation" like spending money as if we were doing life tomorrow in San Quentin. The babes made their choices, and insisted that I had to see these Beanies (I bet). They were so cute, they said, especially Schultzie, the German Shepherd (the Germans again) and Spot.

"I can't live without them," they said. Not them, me!

"Yes, I could," I said.

"No, you can't," they said.

"Yeah, I really could," I said.

"No, you really couldn't," they said, a little more malevolently … or was I imagining it?

"You want these, dad."

"OK, OK," I said, making sure I knew where the exits were. I bought them, and we left; my life now more enriched. I can't say the same for my self-image, however. But the dang things are very cute… and damn the torpedoes.

A Couple of Beanie Baby Stories, From When They Were Littler

(Kindly keep in mind, I started this book a few years ago and the kids are not as emotionally arrested as they seem).

The kids played "Beanie Baby Shoppe" for years. My daughter, Em, was the VP of Merchandising, and my son was the VP of Sales. The reasons for these positions will become clear as we go on. They used discarded cell phones, a cash register with play money, a chair and desk, and a display case.

The Beanies were at the foot of the bed, but the stuff was merchandised: basic assortment (items one always has in stock and are re-orderable); items on "special" (meaning higher margin or with manufacturer's incentives increasing your initial mark-up, plus advertising); and closeouts (items that didn't sell. They'd have "seconds," if they could get their hands on them).

You can't make this up, I'm telling you.

They set the retail prices together, but my daughter – who is about money – was the real product manager. With those kinds of initial mark - ups, I'd be laughed off the planet if I tried something like this: picture a dollar and selling it for a dollar fifty. In their minds, perfectly acceptable. They set the value, and it would be easier to tell Hitler not to invade Russia than to change their minds. You want it, you have to pay, Fräulein! So, that's my daughter.

My son, Alexander, was in charge of the company's return policy. Granted this is more the bailiwick of the finance guys, but he took the responsibility for it since no one else wanted it. The return policy consisted of verbally beating a customer to death for even *suggesting* a return when it was clear there was a *"no return policy."* It was apparently written in stone somewhere in the company's bylaws. And no, there was no copy of this available for your perusal, by the way, or so said my son, the "executive."

This is him on the phone. This conversation really took place, and these are not actors:

"No, I am very sorry, sir, but we do not accept returns."

(Customer pleading, usually me playing this role.) "But sir, I just bought this like … five minutes ago."

"I am very sorry for the inconvenience this has caused you."

(Pause.) "But maybe you'd be interested in one of our specials?"

I do this for a living, and I can't hold a candle to the thick skin and iron will this kid has. Ten years old and better at this than I am. He understands the basic premise of dealing with an irritated customer: change the subject and show new product. Sales 101. It always works, and the thing is, it comes naturally to him. I hate that kid.

And by the way, I still have the world's worst Beanie Baby, with a name something like "Putzie the Mook" … and no prayer of a refund. Great. Just perfect. And quite telling, for several reasons, I might add. Not the least of which is, who the heck knew I was dealing with a ten-year-old Willie Loman? I mean, who knew? Serves me right for helping create him.

Another added bonus of traveling with the kids is getting to hear the conversations between Beanie Babies, when they are bored and tired of sitting in the back seat. (I'm referring to the Beanies, mind you.) These conversations have to be heard to be believed. Listening to them while they converse, shout, persuade, and hondle each other has, on more than one occasion, almost caused me to crash the car. Here's an example (and I apologize in advance):

It was early in the morning. Very early and quiet.

A little too quiet …

The babes were looking out the window. The kids were tired. I was tired, but we had a long trip ahead. But I want to say, those Beanies don't give a hoot how tired you are, I'm telling you. They complain constantly.

Schultzie (as opposed to Schmaltze, the Jewish Beanie), "Oy, I'm tired."

Swoop (the Pelican): "Me too."

Schultzie: "I could use some fuel."

Swoop: "Good idea. Here's some gasoline!"

Schultzie: "Yecchh, that stuff tastes awful!" (You can't make this up.)

Swoop: "OK, I'll put the nozzle here instead!"

Narrator: OK, I didn't want to look, but I could guess. Oh, I could guess. I mean, their median age was 11 and a half.

Schultzie (gratified): "Aaaahhhh. Much better. I feel refreshed."

Narrator: I know it's only 8 am, but I'll have a very dry Stoli martini, straight up. *Now, please …*

My son tends to be the more comical of the two (he played the role of Schultzie). My daughter, the eldest, is deaf. As a result, in this case, she's also very serious. At times, too serious, which is sad. Our little guy, well, when you talk to him, sometimes you think you're speaking to your own father.

Having a deaf child first gave us little guidance on what to expect as a child matures thru her adolescence. It would have been nice to have a guideline but, of course, we didn't. And now as then, we wouldn't have traded Emma for anything. It was an experience we simply had to have, for whatever reason God proposed, and we've always accepted and dealt with it. Simple as that, I'm happy to say.

But as far as my son, "Abraham Lincoln," you can end up laughing your tail off because his remarks can be so pleasantly surprising. One wouldn't expect these things, if we'd had the experience, to come out of a ten-year-old's mouth. No ten year old I ever met was quite like him (of course, I didn't pay attention to kids before I had them). But he can astound you. Some examples:

Alex (talking to me): "Well, *my young friend*, I do know what a vas deferens is … *sadly.*" (This was my first, and also my last, attempt at sex education; let him learn it on the corner like I did.)

When Alex was about seven, the ladies of my neighborhood where sitting on our porch. Lisa said to Al, go upstairs and take a shower. And make sure a soapy part of the wash-cloth touches every part of your body.

One of my neighbor ladies (a very cute one) said, "If you don't do that, Alex, I'm going to wash you."

She didn't mean it *that* way but he took it *that* way. He said, "Somebody pinch me, I must be dreaming."

My boy also has a temper. So I decided (reprising my role as Dad of the Year) to tell him about Dwight Eisenhower's mother. She despaired of young Eisenhower's temper and told him many times that no man could achieve his potential unless he mastered his own emotions. What a great little life lesson to impart: concise, meaningful, using an eminent, historical figure, which, upon telling merely one time, would be forever imprinted on Alex's cerebellum, thereby creating a clone of "Ike," an 'Ike-ette," if you will. Instead, I got more of an Ike – man. He lost his temper later, I referred him back to the life lesson and he said, loudly, "DAD, I AM NO DWIGHT EISENHOWER!"

I have to give him credit at least for having his eminent personages correct.

Lesson #6 in Life

Most of the time with kids, you roll a seven.

I must say that east Texas was everything it was supposed to be. Which, so let's be honest, actually wasn't much. Comparatively, east Texas is lush and green as opposed to an arid landscape, with arthritic looking trees, like Dallas. I love Dallas and really wouldn't want to live anywhere else. It fits, in a lot of ways. Not too crowded, which is a key factor for me. (It doesn't take much for me to feel closed in.) I totally love New York City however, and could live there … if I hit the lottery. And you best hit the lottery to begin to even think of it, because it takes *serious money.* A stupid sandwich is $10. Oh, and the place has raised aggravation to new heights, not previously achieved by Man. (And for you actual Lottery winners who may have had some class somehow grafted onto their genetic material — which they should make a require-ment – there's a sandwich at 21 that costs a thousand dollars.)

Lesson #7 in Life

If you hit The Big One, order one up medium rare, baby, and hold the mayo!

But NYC has a heck of a lot to compensate for high prices, not the least of which is its cultural superiority to any-where else in the USA. I'm not referring to the pledge most people who live there take to be total hedonists and liberal fanatics, but the real culture: art, for example. Europe may have more antiquities and museums brimming with classic paintings, but NYC is close, plus it has everything else I con-sider important … like food.

Lesson #8 in Life

Smearing feces on a painting of the Blessed Virgin Mary or dipping a cross in urine is not art.

The great artists of our past would laugh themselves silly because they know how real works of art come into being[ii]. I particularly loved how one dung "artist" tried to worm his way out of the torrent of negative publicity by saying that in his ancestral homeland, feces was a symbol of fertility and life. Sure. What he really wanted to say was that he was just another no-talent, beret-and-scarf-wearing "artiste" whose honest intent was to smear scheit on the Virgin Mary, since he hated everything about her. Try doing that to a painting of Mohammed. Try *painting* Mohammed. At least be honest about it, OK, dung boy? Maybe one day I'll spew my expectorations onto a canvas and tell everyone I'm going for Jackson Pollock. I'll bet I can get public funding for it and the subsequent accolades regarding what a genius I am.

But let's not forget, New York has food to die for, which I am about. If you eat the steak at Peter Luger[iii] or the seafood at Le Bernardin (I'm told) or simply having a mouth-watering, overstuffed corned beef sandwich at the Carnegie Deli as an appropriate finish to an afternoon well-spent at the Met, if that moves you … come on! You know you're on to something. And you can't do that anywhere else in the US that I know of. Only in the Apple, baby. Picasso and … sprouts? I don't think so, do you? And don't even say LA, which is a wasteland in every sense of the word. Unless you really like sprouts, organic wheat bread, and melon served with everything. Hey wait a minute, call my kids. It's is heaven on earth, momma style![iv]

But Texas has been my home for 25 years. My kids were born here. The people you meet every day are nice. It's relatively quiet, except for the occasional gunshot on New Year's Eve. However, it has a quality that mystifies me. Namely, what draws people to it, especially at the beginning? I mean, I can barely stand Houston *now*.

Imagine, people came to New York (from their own hell on earth, I'm sure), crossed that rough country that was America then, and avoided slow death:

... by starvation,

... by arrow,

... by pestilence,

... or by falling into a canyon,

... by drowning in some river,

... by having a tree fall on them,

... by being shot by some deranged person who went crazy during the journey from not eating enough organics,

... all while not failing to mention some un-nameable diseases that ate your extremities and rotted your brain. If you survived that, the word lucky doesn't even apply to you.

And yet you came from Germany, or Sweden, or Ireland, or Mother Russia and saw:

... this sun-baked,

... die from thirst,

... fry your adrenals and sauté your liver place,

and said, "This is for me, Horst / Lars / Paddy / Irving. Even better, there ain't no Jews here. Yippee!"

The big issue still remained that you were drawn to this ... place, and they didn't have a chicken fried steak yet.[v]

My barber used to tell me how much Texas history he had to learn. I was amazed. I learned very little Pennsylvania history as a kid, except by way of studying the American Revolution. This turned out to be a good thing. Except for cheese steaks and those 4 o'clock in the morning french fry sandwiches in Pittsburgh ... yeah? What else is there, the Amish? Now my kids learn all this cool Texas stuff. The Battle of San Jacinto. Who the guys were at the Alamo. The proud traditions of the state, which are quite real. Lyndon Baines Johnson. OK, I made that last one up because a bigger hunka' brisket had never before existed.

But I understand the need to celebrate the individual initiative that created this civilization out of a roughhewn wilderness. That must have taken some major "want to," as they say down here (and maybe a little too much exposure to the blistering sun). Turning *that* chicken %^)% into *this* chicken salad was no small feat. I don't claim to understand the mindset, but that strength of character is worthy of praise. I wouldn't have done it. I'd have taken one look at this place and beat a path back to whence I came. Back to Pennsylvania, if you can believe that. Pennsylvania? I mean what, the Amish? There ain't nothin' else, OK? I understood the Texas mentality that, in a nutshell, appears to be getting some property and fencing it off. Who cares if it's the size of a laundry room?

Dateline: Somewhere East of Tyler and West of Hope (Arkansas)

The kids were quiet again. I looked into the rear view and was reminded of a simple fact that always manages to fascinate me: I saw two babies, and they were both from me.

I recalled all the times I'd fantasized about what my kids, if I ever had any (and I swore I wouldn't have any, or a wife either) would be like, and here they were. I should note that I was never one of those predictable types who, once having a kid, was overcome and overwhelmed with new emotion. Namely, that there was actually something in the world other than one's self (see: Star, Movie). I knew it was great and beyond the pale, but I was never one to see only myself. God gave me this quality from as far back as I can recollect.

I remember when the delivery room staff handed me my daughter (who was beautiful and not crying at all), and that handing her over freaked me out totally. To be honest, she scared the bejeebees out of me. There was this fragile little thing and what if dorky me dropped her? Holy Smoly! I started looking for the exits. I thought I was going to have a heart attack, and they'd end up working on me instead. Where were her real parents so I could give her back?

I calmed myself and said, "Hello, precious little baby." (She had big ears sticking out of her head.) Then I handed her to her mother as fast as I could. It was about two or three days before I got used to her. I kept looking at that gorgeous face (after the swelling from the forceps delivery went down; before that: "Ultimate Fighting"). Her face hasn't changed all that much since. But then she had a flabby belly I couldn't seem to get enough of. And these teeny feet I had to prevent myself from snacking on. I was madly in love with that little "moo moo." I wondered how all the atoms suspended in the ether coalesced to form this emotion inside me, so deeply and so quickly.

I wondered, what would my children look like, ulti-mately? It should have been so easy to see, if I'd a brain in my head. My dad's genes dominate everything. He had four kids, and we all look exactly like he did. I have two babies, and they both look exactly like me. My wife, who's exquisite, says she was there only for the stretch marks. My babes are beautiful. Without false humility, it looks *a lot* better on them than it does on me, which is yet another miracle wrought by God (and thanks for it).

OK, so I knew something was up with Em at nine months. No one would listen to me. I thought she was deaf. She talked funny; sounded like a person who couldn't hear. I'm tuned into nuances of personality such as these and am ever vigilant (probably stems from paranoia).

Her doctor …

My bride …

Her day care people …

My mother …

My dad …

My sisters …

My wife's mother …

No one would listen to me. I don't love frustration, OK? I also don't love it when my hair turns gray, or falls out, or both. As I write this, I note that every gray hair on my head is from worrying about this baby.

When Em was a little over two, when we could, we ran a test on her. The result?

Deaf as a post …

Thank you. Apologies accepted from everyone. My wife took me aside especially to say she was sorry for being wrong. It wasn't necessary. Our arguments about Emma's hearing amounted to about five minutes totally. Now, we had to deal with it.

So, what have I garnered from all this? It proved to me that I'm totally, and to this day, wired into my baby. She can't have a thought in another room that I don't know about. The atoms in the ether came together to form this bond between us that exists on a molecular level. I know it's from God, because no one can really explain how it happens, even with adoptive families. But another part of me that allows me to communicate telepathically with Emma is I have an interest about other people's behavior. Why they do what they do, and what is the cause? I've made, unconsciously, a study of it. It gives me some freedom. However, I can't help but note with profound irony that it had abandoned me royally *of late*. But even that served a purpose: don't draw conclusions and, thereby, feel safe around people who aren't a living match to at least 19 of your chromosomes.

So while we're on this road trip, my baby, who has a little hearing, is sitting in the back of the car with the CD player headphones behind her ears and directly on her hearing aids. She looks like a pilot who's pushed her headset back so she can hear someone talking.

She was singing, which I guess beat staring out the car window at Arkansas. She sings like someone who can't hear their own voice … which is painful for the rest of us. Sort of like taking a cat and putting it your blender. Screechy, if you know what I mean. Yet I detect in her singing voice some real talent – but she can't hear herself sing. As compensation, she plays the piano – with no hearing, mind you – like Mozart. Go figure how *that* happened. Partly my wife riding herd on her, I assure you. Yee hah !

There's a general myth about hearing aids, that they give you hearing. They don't. They amplify the sound, where possible, to stimulate what little hearing you have. But they don't help you hear like you and I do. Em has no range beyond the lowest base sounds. So the hearing aid geniuses – and I'm serious, for once – designed a hearing aid that brings *all* sound into that range. The first time she wore them, it rained on the roof of the car while we went home, and she heard that "sound." She was taken aback by it and pretty excited. She didn't think rain made a lot of noise when it hit something. She was amazed and happy. It was a revelation to her. I stayed pretty cool. But when I got back to my bedroom, I cried like a two year old. I never think about rain. I only think about my baby.

Lisa and I took her all over Dallas to specialists to see if we could remedy her handicap. That's right, *her handicap*. No spinning here or PC euphemisms. It's a hearing world, and if you don't hear, *you are handicapped*. Surprisingly, she survived her mom and dad calling her handicap what it is: *a handicap*. We checked out cochlear implants (CIs) with the ENT who was a pioneer in the field ($40,000, then, and no insurance covers it). He couldn't wait to cut her. Once we reined him in, we discovered she was not a candidate. OK.

Lesson #9 in Life

In the world out there, they make no concessions
for handicapped people, nor should they go out of
their way to do so.

Having a lower urinal in men's restrooms today is hardly a giant leap for mankind and handicapped people. If my daughter was a candidate for a CI, and if it would give her a leg up in her current situation, they'd be drilling holes in her head right now with an antique hand drill, if need be.

Lisa and I anguished over what we could do for Em. We later learned it really had to come from her, with help from us. Besides, we have yet to see a CI, for example, make a talking, well-functioning person of a deaf child. With the kids we have seen, and with the cost at $40,000, you'd be better off buying land. Adults are another matter; people who've heard fully before. Then, CIs can be the miracle that's their design.

Oh, we did some serious looking into remedies or potential remedies, looking for causes (hers is genetic). The Deaf community, with whom we interacted for about an hour, gave us less than zero help and guidance. They are so forward-thinking they believe CIs are Nazi experimentation. You can't make this up. They're also the most dysfunctional and angry group of people we've ever met (besides Nazis). They all seem to hate each other (like Nazis). Hang around them long enough, and you'll be looking to open a main vein at the first opportunity. We kept our kid away from them. So, what happens when she's not regularly with her own kind, away from this level of comfort the Deaf community claim she'd sorely miss? She's awesome and excels at everything (has my brains). Emma:

takes pre-AP or AP classes in a regular public school, simultaneously watching the teacher and an interpreter and following the class material …

plays the piano like an ace …

took the PSATs in 6th grade …

made National Honor Society in high school …

and in 10th grade is getting college letters of interest from places like the University of Chicago. Yes, *that* University of Chicago. And they don't know she's deaf; they just think she's really smart. It's 99% her and 1% her mother and I. Collectively, we won't let her fade away. Because I'm here to tell you, in that world, the deaf world, it happens all the time. How many deaf people do you know?

An example: sometimes I'll be in a restaurant, and a guy will come over and hand out a card with a lapel pin, let's say, and ask for a donation. The card he gives you (with my interest in being completely politically correct hereby noted, women do this, too), says he's deaf and *has* to do this. The first couple of times this happened to me, I signed the following phrases in English, not ASL(the deaf version of slang):

"What are you doing?"

"You're giving a bad name to deaf people."

"What the *heck* is wrong with you?" (I used a slightly different word …).

"Go away, you're hacking me off" (my favorite "sign," which we *all* know).

Patrons may stare at me (who's the iceberg?) and sometimes ask what I said (as if that particular sign needs an interpreter.) Sometimes I explain that some people *really are* charlatans. Next time, maybe he'll have a baby, in a papoose on his back, to get the full effect intended.

If people still don't get it, I ask them to picture this: he's handing out cards and asking for money, and my daughter's applying to the University of Chicago. You do the math. Adversity makes you stronger, "Enabler Breath." And I can *sign that phrase, too,* using *other* words that fit my emotional state, at those moments.

In any case, I've cried many a tear over the fact my babe *can't* hear. Deafness is a truly horrible, pernicious thing.

Worse than blindness. Even Ray Charles said this during an interview. Deafness affects every single aspect of your life:

socialization …

learning …

psychological development…

emotional maturity …

Did I miss anything? If I did, add it to the list. Try calling 911 and be unable to hear the person on the other end of the line. This is one small example. But we can't allow surrender to it. We're morally obligated to do this. Period.

So what did God ask of me in all this? Try to be a little more patient. I'm a person who loves efficiency and hates its opposite. I count the steps to the car to figure out the best way of getting there. Another part of my insane efficiency is hating to repeat myself. Wonderful quality to have with a deaf child. A child who, you might say, works "the system" to help herself and aggravate me. Sometimes I blow my cork. This, she always manages to hear. People dead for 1,000 years can hear me then. Last time I blew my cork, the US Geological Survey called to make sure their seismic readings were not South America crashing into Africa. Yes, it's that loud. Regrettably. My wife is building a shelter to run into the next time it happens (when my wife's family argues, you need the ears of a bat to hear anything. And then they can't stop talking about what a horrible blowout they just had, which is truly hilarious). This was baby #1.

Then there's baby # 2, the salesman I mentioned before. I call him Junius, sort of an abbreviation of Junior, since he is a clone of me. Granted, his name is Alexander, named after my late mother and Louis, after the black woman, Willie Lou, who loved me totally and unconditionally as a child. He may look like me, but he's funnier than I ever hope to be. We've called him, at various times in his life:

BoBo Head

Booger

Alphonse

Alley Cat (his current handle)

Squeaky

Fonz

GooGoose

Muchka

Beans

Pinky

Minky

Blinky

Buzzard Beak

Baby Shaina (sort of a "new Yiddish" kind of thing)

Wart Boy (you can figure that out)

And Soy Bean and / or Burrito Brain

We were expecting a girl, actually hoping for one. Then he came out ... a month early ... at 5:34 am, and I've hated him ever since. That was too danged early for me. My wife and I were so calloused to labor, we went to the hospital at 9 pm, and I lay on the hospital room sofa and went to sleep. And my wife was perfectly OK with it, she couldn't have cared less. If she needed me, she reasoned, she could let me know (and what on earth, really, could I have done? I didn't have the narcotics or I'd have taken them). All I could do was pace her breathing like they teach you in the *beyond* useless Lamaze class ... while she tried to rip my eyeballs out until the epidural. So I did what I do best: I took a nap.

The little one, on his first day of life, kept us up all night, creating a sleep pattern that's more or less continued for years, though he gets up now and doesn't bother us. He used to walk in and go, "I AM AWAKE NOW!."

And I would sleepily say something like, "WHO GIVES A $#@%? GET OUTTA' HERE." You know, warm and loving, after five years of *no sleep*. Sometimes he actually left and went back to his room … after we threw hot water on him.

Anyway, he turned out to be so different from Emma, in the sense that he was this new addition to our family, and it took some getting used to. Over the years, I've often caught myself looking at him doing something, watching TV or looking out the window, and I'm in awe of him. He's one beautiful kid and funny as all get out, as we say back at the farm. I'm talking really hilarious.

Somebody pinch me, I must be dreaming.

He spent about six weeks in kindergarten, and they moved him up to first grade. He managed to fit right in. The rest is history. And he's darn fun to be around.

Chapter Three

Tennessee: "I'm Going to Graceland, Graceland, in Memphis, Tennessee" (not really)

We made it to Memphis the first day. Not much going on there, except it started to get real pretty the closer we got to Tennessee. We stayed the night and left the next morning. We could easily have gone for BBQ to someplace great, but we were on a self-imposed schedule. For what reason, I don't know.

After the babes were nicely tucked into their beds at the LaQuinta Suites (and after they approved the room, which I am NOT making up), I lay in my bed (I insisted on having the king, which they relinquished to me … after a brief argument, of course). I started thinking about the recent events and how ravaged I was emotionally. I tried to sort out my frustrations and anger that seemed to be consuming me.

The babes didn't know it, though they did share their opinions about the matter: They'd say things like, "I thought you were friends, and that stunk what she did to you, dad."

I told them I'd never do the types of things I was accused of because they related to a "power trip," something in which I have rarely, if ever, indulged myself. I also told them I'd never lie to them about something like this; it was too important a lesson for them to learn from. If it hurt *me* in the process, too bad.

In any case, I took the time each night of this trip to come to grips with my place in all of it. Slowly, almost imperceptibly, it began to sort itself out[vi]. I had help, mind you, people like a friend and business associate who stood by me and helped me through it. And some prayer when I could stop the flood of thoughts long enough to concentrate. Remember, I said in the Epigram that I was in the boat? Boy, was I ever. Faith that everything would turn out OK seemed like a very faraway prospect from the precipice I occupied. I truly knew it would occur, but the horizon looked awful murky from where I stood.

Early the next morning, after I approved what the kids were eating (sort of), we headed to Nashville and The Hermitage to see Old Hickory, or what was left of him. On the way, somewhere along the line, we saw a sign that pointed to Shiloh National Military Park. Now this was something I really wanted to see. I'd never been to a Civil War battlefield before, and I'd been a Civil War buff in my youth. I asked the kids if they wanted to go to The Hermitage or Shiloh. They said, "The Hermitage." So we went to Shiloh.

Lesson #10 in Life

Never let anyone under 21 vote for anything. Maybe 31.
They are basically unformed.

(See: TV, M)

Lesson #10a in Life

Never, I mean never, give your kids a choice in anything.
Parenthood ain't a democracy. Let them vote and you're
dead, even if it is the type of ice cream they want.

We drove through the back roads to get to Shiloh. Lots of woods, pretty colors. Verdurous, if you will (thank you, Rupert Brooke). We bought some souvenirs and did the map tour. It was unbelievable, in a sense. Woods were everywhere, with signs marking the positions of the various regiments and companies, monuments to individuals and battalions, and the states from which they came. How the heck could you fight a battle, in woods like this, and have any idea whatever what the hey was going on? Yet ultimately, I was to see this very scenario in many places we visited. We tread where many had tread before and stood where thousands had bled, possibly right beneath our feet. We walked where many had died painful deaths, in numbers unimaginable by any standard. Some who touched this hallowed ground did not die, possibly to die later or not die at all. Maybe even survived, in a physical sense. The psychological trauma must have been staggering and impossible to truly survive. I stood, with my babies, where they did. Keep in mind, you could only mentally visualize these events. But such strength these images had in the imagining. What the heck must that have been like?

One hundred and forty odd years ago, the very woods would have been shooting at me. Cannon shell would have exploded all around me, spreading shrapnel and creating a killing circle that vaporized anything in its deadly radius. You could only hope, I guess, that you were about 1 millimeter outside that life-extinguishing blast or one inch away from that small hunk of minie (a little ball of metal shaped like a pea) designed to remove your head and put it in your lap.

And then you would have been ordered to move forward through this fusillade and contact, for possibly the first time ever, whatever potential cataclysm awaited you. Expecting, realistically, no better than a 50/50 outcome. All your life came down to one millisecond. How could you prepare for that? Would you live? Or experience an explosive death and burial in some anonymous grave, with everyone else dumped on top of you, all dignity and honor taken? (As if getting blown to bits or shot through the heart wasn't enough.) One second, alive and sweating. And the next?

What is death like when there's no transition available to you?, I thought. Please tell me that God guides you through this. "Please," I whispered to myself (the kids were elsewhere just then). I felt so damn morose. Was I experiencing those moments vicariously? So many lives were instantly extinguished. They left energy behind, they had to, and maybe this was what I was experiencing. But I'm not trying to sound like some carnival "Contactor of the Dead." I'm told that scenes of great carnage, as this surely was, bring out this elemental response in people. My guess is that's true. This sounds only natural. Yes, I have to believe God never leaves you for one billionth of a second, since with Him, there is no time, and therefore, transition is an imaginary, fabricated thing. Right? Actually, I truly do believe this.

But my mind raced with all these thoughts in the first 15 minutes at Shiloh. The events had me firmly in their grip. And at first, I didn't think of God. I mean, how could anyone? Dead people were thrown into a pile and left to rot 140 years ago. I wouldn't wish that on anyone. My God doesn't immediately spring to mind until I come to my senses and see very clearly His vision. He was very much here, I knew, and everywhere else. But please don't ask me to explain it to you. At least not then, at Shiloh.

We finished our side trip to Shiloh with a trip to the artifacts and memorabilia shop next door to the battlefield and picked up a couple of things. We met a fellow who later became the war memorabilia expert on PBS's "Antiques Roadshow." He explained to us that the state had recently chopped down the tree beneath which Albert Sydney Johnston lay as he died (he was one of the Confederate generals and quite famous). They chopped it down for some reason I still can't quite understand. The tree was quite an attachment to the past. And it was chopped down. Now Johnston's tree is lighting someone's fireplace. That says it all, doesn't it?

Somehow we realized it was late afternoon, and the kids, though at first reluctant, had a great time at Shiloh. They learned from the whole experience. But we had to make tracks now, in order to please daddy further. We were going to the Jack Daniel's Distillery! I had to see that place. My kids, who were really running this trip (let's be honest), were extremely lukewarm to the idea of going to Lynchburg. But damn the torpedoes, full speed ahead, so said I. There was a bottle of sour mash "jes awaitin' on ol' dad." Besides, I'd invoked Life Lesson #10a, and that was all there was to it. To be really frank, I don't drink that brown turpentine, but I sure loved the sound of what I was getting myself into and "jes a talkin thisa way."

We had to take back roads to get there. Not always the fastest way to go but, for sure, the prettiest. Twice in my life getting off the main roads has paid off in spades for me. The first time was when I diagonally crossed the state of Virginia in the fall. You want to talk about one of the most beautiful sights you can behold? Well, that was surely one. As I drove, I couldn't help but wonder what all these mountain type men were doing by the side of the road all thru the trip. With guns, too. I thought they must be pretty State's rights in ol' Virginny, until I got a clue later. It was the first day of hunting season. I'm a city boy, OK? I don't hunt. Deer scare me. They can bite, can't they?

The second time I went off the main road, I was on the Autobahn going about 300 kph headed for Bavaria. It was raining pretty hard, which, believe it or not, deterred no one from passing me like I was standing still. I could have been in "park" for all it mattered. I was in a Renault and the hamsters were really working their treadmills. One minute I was cruising and looking in the rear view. The next minute, some Dutch lunatic in a Porsche was about two inches from my rear bumper. So close I might have counted his nose hairs, but really couldn't because I was already distracted from having soiled myself out of fear. I couldn't get out of his way fast enough, for him or for me. He blinked his high beams at me and I swear, to this day, he got behind me faster than the light itself did. I got off the road, drove about a mile, looked up, and saw the most tremendous monastery I'd ever seen attached to the side of a mountain. No more main roads for me, then or at any other time. I guess I have that wooden-shod Dutch guy to thank for all the wonderful side trips I've had since.

Crazy, canal-skating, windmill worshipper.

As I drove through Tennessee, our car seemed to be alone. The trees and hills formed a tunnel, and I was reminded of the tunnel I imagine exists sometime in the future, which each of us must traverse when called to our fate. It was getting later in the day and slightly dark, made more so by the landscape. We were going through this living tunnel after experiencing the cataclysms of Shiloh, though long ago, still somewhat present in the "ether." It wasn't eerie but, in fact, rather calming. I thought this a little strange and pleasant at the same time. I can only hope my future traversal feels as comforting. And goes north i.e. to heaven.

I spotted something on the road as I blew through the countryside. I drove past and turned around in some country boy's driveway (by the look on his face, he hadn't had a visitor in quite some time; he probably thought I was the ATF or something). Anyway, it was a turtle, about six inches long, just moseying across this two lane road. I assume it was moseying. What else do turtles really do? Shuffle, I guess. Maybe he was going full bore and it just looked like lolly-gagging. I was amazed I could come up with so many adjectives describing the motion of a turtle. I can't believe how many neurons I've dedicated to schmucky stuff like that.

We did a turtle intervention. It was the highlight of the day. It was a beautiful black and tan color. (Why is everything in my life reduced to alcohol?[vii]) My son took him to the other side of the road and put him in the grass. We felt pretty good about ourselves. We basked in the good feelings generated by helping our fellow earthly creatures. Then, we thought of two things:

1.   We were sort of *guessing* he was moseying to *that* side of the road. He was sort of cooped up in his shell, aiming in sort of a lateral way.

2.   We didn't screw up his life so bad he got killed trying to make right what we made wrong, with our good intentions.

We can only hope he lived to be a grandfather and is praising our names to his relatives; "big white car, dent in muffler, take grandpa, make right!"... or else he became a tiny grease spot covering the road to Hooterville.

I'll say one thing about the turtle: our little foray with him made me late to Lynchburg by 15 minutes, and I was hell for leather trying to get there. Fifteen minutes from that delicious corn whiskey tended by bearded Uncle Jack himself. So close, yet so far; inches from the brass ring. Smooth, silky, smoky ... and instead I became a full-fledged member of PETA at the urging of my kids, so I could feel good about land mollusks; a species I never gave a single thought to prior to my hillbilly excursion. Actually, it really disturbed my carefully laid plans *which I hate*. When we stopped to eat that night, out of a sorta wimpy revenge, I had snapper soup. I can only hope it was his uncle or something.

The little, arachnid-eatin', shell-sheddin' reptile.

We spent the night at a nice hotel. My kids don't know any other kind. Even if it's a LaQuinta, it has to be the only suite they have. OK, it's my fault but I want a nice place to lay my head every night 'cause I'm tired, Lord knows. Bare bones don't cut it for me. I like nice appointments. For those who disagree, I offer my usual mantra: so sue me.

My kids started doing something very sweet in the morning for me, on this day and each day that followed. I'd sleep while they went to eat (where's mom?!), and they'd bring me back black coffee, scrambled eggs, bacon, and toast on a tray. How sweet is that? They did this every day during our trip, and I loved them for it. Cholesterol being of no consideration, of course. Maybe they had a secret plan …

Chapter Four

Oak Ridge, Tennessee:
"Can you say, 'BA BOOM'?"

I saw Oak Ridge on the map and couldn't resist going there. This is where they helped develop the A bomb. It's a subject that's always fascinated me. Not the moral implications of using it in WW2, because they are non-existent, but the geniuses who worked on the darn thing(s). At the University of Chicago, sometime before the war or right at its start, a group of these guys sat in a room and discussed critical mass. In other words, when the build-up of atoms smashing into each other would cause a bomb to go **"BA BOOM!"** J. Robert Oppenheimer, not a well-known person at that point, sat in the back of the room and calculated, on a piece of paper with a pencil, what critical mass would be. No calculator. Just a pencil. And he wasn't the only one doing it. Present were the Hall of Fame scientists of that era (or any other): Enrico Fermi and Niels Bohr, to name a couple. During WW2 Bohr kept his precious stash of "heavy water" (a molecule with an extra neutron or something needed to make the bomb operate properly) in his fridge sealed in some beer bottles. This was in Denmark, and all thru the Nazi occupation, if you can believe it. These must have been the *only* beers in all of Europe:

those pinheaded …

pretzel-munchin' …

spaetzle-slingin' …

forever-marchin'…

"die for the cause'n" …

fire-lighting …

sausage stuffers …

didn't drink.

Because, after all, that's what they were known for: guzzling beer and killing Jews. Nice people. Too bad we didn't have the bomb in time (we didn't) to drop it on those vermin; right on Der Führer's bunker. Bullseye! Take that, you Charlie Chaplin wannabe! And this one's for you, Goebbels.

Ya' anti-social, little … reptile

I was really looking forward to seeing all the exhibits at Oak Ridge and basking in our ultimate victory. The drive was magnificent and that more than made up for the fact … the place was closed when we got there. Oh well, a small victory for the enemy. Seems like my timing, on this trip at least, has been on their side. The little, knudel-makin', book burners.

"Well kids," I said, "I'm looking at the map. So, do you want to see a cavern maybe?"

"How far?," the 40 inch curmudgeon asked. (I would get this for the rest of the trip).

"Great, I'm glad you agree," I said. "Let's go see a cavern."

Cavern Hunting, But First …
Dateline: Chickamauga Battlefield

In the pavilion, a giant electric map illuminated the main room. I say illuminated because it did it on two levels: it showed the troop movements via different moving colors on the map and illuminated the patrons (us), so we could understand the scope of the battle differently than what a car tour provided. For once, I got a clear picture of what the blazes was going on. I couldn't get this perspective from ground level, like a foot soldier. But from above, I could clearly get it, without the hindrances of battlefield smoke, cannon noise, and general death-inducing mayhem (and with an iced tea in my hand). I got a relatively good idea of who was doing what and to whom. And it wasn't pretty. I'm still mystified, to this day, how any general could make strategic moves with all this going on, which could possibly make any sense and affect positively the outcome. But they did: Lee, Grant, Jackson, Sherman, Johnston, to name a few. These were very intelligent and brave men who I imagine, with today's armament, could really wreck some havoc. Nevertheless, they still mystify me. I can't look at "ground" and have it mean a dang thing to me. Even if it just had cows on it. My wife understands how that particular system works. I don't. They just eat grass, expel grass, go tinky, and give milk. And taste delicious when cooked, medium rare, right?

Actually, we took the car tour on our own the night before, because the site was closed until the morning (the Nazis again). We drove at dusk, in a slight rain. It was kind of spooky, and I couldn't imagine living in those conditions under the best of circumstances. As we followed the various paths and read the stone markers, it was continually proved to me that there was no perspective except by using the big electric map. After discussing this, the kids and I agreed it was much better to remain above it, in as many ways as possible.

If you read the accounts of these battles or listen to them on the tour CD, another item becomes very clear picture: Abe Lincoln must have been the most frustrated person since me as a teenager. It seemed that the Yankees continually cut and ran at the slightest provocation, even if they were winning. I'll say that the Yankee general, George Thomas, the "Rock of Chickamauga," must have been inspired by something pretty monumental when he said something like "Retreat? The heck with you." It must have been nice for a northerner to see once in a while, because it appeared to happen so sparingly. Poor Lincoln must have thought he'd been sold out.

Until Grant showed up. He understood one fundamental thing: total annihilation. He promised to do it. a pact he made with the enemy. One piece of scholarship I've read (in a book by McFeeley called *Grant*) says Grant actually didn't possess some overweening quality that made him great, though he was. Upon scouring the various parts of his life, nothing jumps out. Napoleon understood the supply chain like no one ever before, Washington had the patience to wait out the British, MacArthur a gift for faking out his adversary. Grant had none of these virtues. He did want to win, however, and there's something very American about the boy from Galena. Personally, I love the guy. And I was rooting for his side, just so you know.

Bristol Caverns in Bristol, Tennessee

It looked like used trailers were lining the narrow road to the caverns. The landscape was starting to get me a little worried about the prospects. How wrong was I? The trip to the caverns was beautiful: small towns, with their storybook town squares; little local stores; war memorials; wraparound porches on Prairie Revival houses; the part of America I love with all my heart. This is the America that I think represents us best. Yes, I know it has its problems, but at least it appears less complicated, with a heritage clearly intact. I see nothing wrong with this at all, in fact, I see it as enviable. I may be proved wrong, but I can't see how all things being equal, it wouldn't be a good place to start for someone, if they couldn't have what I did. I could spend my life visiting places like this and living the Norman Rockwell life, if even to a small degree.

Our tour guide was 18-year-old Candace. And as is customary when my kids are with me, people seem to drop everything and take care of only us. We took the tour of the caverns, just the four of us. The whole experience was so special and unique to me because as we went through the place, Candace had to turn off the lights. We saw the underground river, the stalactites and stalagmites, and the Indian burial ground (which scared the liquid out of my youngest). By the time we were finished, my kids were best friends with Candace and requested an exchange of addresses. She was a sweet kid, and my babes still talk about her.

The caverns were literally in the owner's backyard. It was awesome, since I hadn't really been in a place like this before. I couldn't imagine one day digging a flower garden and falling into this thing accidentally, which is how, if I recall, it was discovered.

Again, the point of the whole trip was for me to get away for awhile and have the babes come with me. They had a chance to see things, like Bristol, and would be better for it. I could see only good as a result. However, the company insisted, and I agreed, to keep in contact and report my progress, in whatever form that took. There were a lot of long hours on the road when the kids weren't making me laugh or making me angry over silly stuff. I had time to think, and as much as I tried to distract myself from my current situation, I couldn't all the time. My emotions seemed to swing like a pendulum, from anger to melancholy.

The company insisted, possibly for legal reasons (I didn't look into it), that I see a psychiatrist because I "wasn't myself."[viii] I was tired, I'll grant you. What they perceived as "not being myself" was due to living within a difficult business environment, waiting to be eviscerated. I was on guard, which is my nature, and therefore the issue was *me*. Right. This was complicated by a slightly twisted individual, a bubble left of center, with a moment of power. The accusation was everything! All of this put me on the road to wherever I was bound.

Whenever I checked in with the company, I got information that I didn't expect to hear (because I expect people to act without malice, though some did). I heard of plots and subplots, apparent motivations, and real motives. And something began to take shape in my mind. It was this: whom do you trust? I am, I guess, a deep person, *but not a complicated one*. I expect everyone else to be the same way. I've always been this way; what you see is what you get. I've lived with the obvious negatives of this attitude – in business — but they'd always been manageable; worth the problems, until now. I was in the big leagues, if you could call it that, since, on so many levels, it was actually the little league.

But I was in this "game" and had to prevail. I'd literally taken up the mantle of some folks in distress, which was one element of the whole episode that I haven't mentioned, and it caused me later to pay dearly. I didn't offer lip service like I see people do all the time. This was an important life lesson: this is a world where, for good or ill, we're compelled in the end to make compromises, despite the rightness or wrongness of an issue. Were these compromises made for business purposes, where emotion played only a small role? Or were these compromises made for expediency, where the goal was more important than the journey? Or, was it really not all that important, and we needed to move ahead and forget about the whole thing? I never found out. All I know is I wouldn't give up my moral high ground. I had no say in the matter really, but I refused to fold. That was something I simply wouldn't / won't do.

Natural Bridge, Virginia

We stopped at a hotel in Roanoke, and once again it was the type with suites. I made the error of giving my kids the guidebooks to read in the back seat. The most crucial thoughts in their decisions were did the hotel have a pool? Was it indoors or out? What time did it close? How deep was it? Did it have a diving board?

I asked, "Where's my gun?"

No matter what we did that day, whether it was visiting Arlington, going thru yet another cavern, or walking over a battlefield, when I asked them if it was as cool as I thought it was they always uniformly responded the same way. "Well yeah, dad, it is. But what time did you say the pool closed again?" You can't make this up.

When we got to Natural Bridge, Virginia, I wasn't prepared to be impressed. It was a natural wonder, so OK.

I was blown away by it ....

Compared to everything we'd seen and everything we were going to see, this was about the coolest thing I'd *ever* seen. Even the "ingrates" were mesmerized.

Why? I'm not sure. A beautiful meandering creek ran downhill into the river, and the river had created the bridge over eons of time. The creek made a babbling brook sound that went right through me. That little piece alone moved me. Looking back, the sound calmed me, something all the Thorazine and martinis in the world couldn't currently do. I'm not a nature boy, though I fully appreciate its finer qualities. I don't, however, spend any time camping or living off the land in any way. I don't hunt, except for a good Philly cheese steak outside of Philly. I find repulsive the thought of sitting in a boat on a slimy lake waiting for a fish to strike. I loathe fish. I'd have to be sedated to do that.[ix] In fact, I'd insist. The funny thing is, I can shoot like Davy Crockett; I know something about fishing; I can lay brick, I can do all of this manly-man stuff. I simply choose not to. I want room service, in bed with my wife, in a snazzy hotel. To me, that is living. The other things I consider nature's lesser qualities, like comparing bass lures.

As you approach the Bridge via the path by the river, the enormity of this natural wonder makes you a little dizzy. As you look up, you're simply overwhelmed emotionally. It makes you feel insignificant, quite frankly, but you feel compelled to be there. We hated to leave and bumped into the metal seats as we left. We kept turning around to re-experience the whole thing again.

We followed the trail to the Natural Bridge Caverns. The kids were anxious to go. They'd had so much fun with Candace, they couldn't wait to see this cave. There was about a 300 foot descent, maybe more, into the cavern at, like, a ten degree angle. I started to hate it, because I found the whole idea of going down into the ground a little creepy... until the 30 kindergarteners and their parents started to distract me. Kids are cute and I love them … now. I wasn't in the mood for their six-year-old questions right then, especially when I was clearly confined with no way out. And they were a little out of control. My kids were very polite.

The rule about tour guides dropping everything didn't hold true … during the first 15 minutes. After that, he spent the rest of his time with us and the kinders followed while *we* explained what he told *us*. This was a very cool little arrangement, with the appropriate monetary remuneration following thereafter. I'm waiting for his Christmas card, which I'm confident I'll be getting.

The Virginia people did it right, I'm here to tell you.ˣ Nothing low rent about this whole set-up. I can't wait to go back, for no other reason then to see God's handwriting again. When I emerged from that cave, I felt like Lazarus rising from the dead, in more ways than one.

But Lazarus, luckily for him, didn't have those kids to contend with.

There was an overload, if that was possible, of beautiful scenery to behold in Virginia. We found ourselves climbing up one side of a mountain, only to descend down the other on a cobble stone road. More than once. And people drove very slowly, and I wasn't going "New York" on them. I was making progress. Deeply woodsy. Clear, with farm houses dotting the landscape. Can't beat that with a stick. No wonder General Lee loved this place.

Periodically, it rained torrentially. I thought I was in New Guinea. I sort of felt sorry for the drivers behind us as they were getting pelted. We eventually stopped at New Market Battlefield.

New Market Battlefield

By the standards of Chickamauga and Shiloh, it's a tiny piece of land; only a couple of acres. We bought the usual trinkets (and did at all the stops we made: hats, pins, decals, miniature guns). We were told the history of New Market, where about 200 students from VMI, held off a Yankee battalion or some such number. The Yankees retreated to Washington (did we actually *win* this war?). Some very young kids died that day.

The field was small enough to really get a picture of what happened. It also was a field and not closed in with trees like the other battlefields. I'm guessing, as I write this, that the sense of the battles' strategies was important only to me. Maybe a lot of people go to the battlefields, see the relics, and move on without much deep thought about it. I also have nothing against this mindset. But I have an insatiable curiosity about terrain and what it does to the flow of battle. I wonder if I would have attacked in the same way, looking at the ground and recalling my available numbers. I know that professional soldiers study history and draw relevant conclusions on how to prepare for battle. I also know there are those who don't read military history and paid dearly, which is sometimes good. (See: winter, Hitler attacks in).

Napoleon found out the hard way when he tried invading Russia in the winter (though the retreat may not have been the shambles history has judged it to be, or so goes recent scholarship). Thank goodness Hitler thought he was a modern-day Frederick Barbarossa. He was actually more like a Mrs. Barbarossa. But he was still a genuine troublemaker of the highest order.[xi] He killed himself because he had no guts. Would have been nice to have him tour the country in a monkey cage like he wanted to do to Clark Gable, if he ever caught him (or so thought Gable). But if Hitler was in the monkey cage, then we all could have thrown manootz on him. For that, I would have paid *big money*. Probably all I have.

Anyway, I really tried to get a sense of the Civil War, like I would do if I was at Okinawa or Normandy. I'm not so interested in the relics really, and I'm told I never actually have been. My parents told me I was fodder for many a cocktail party conversation the last time I was interested in relics. We were at Valley Forge, and I was fascinated, I'm told, by the pyramid-shaped stacks of cannon balls welded together that lined the battlefield. So I asked my parents how come George Washington's balls were stuck together. My parents were very hip and laughed their buns off for years over that one. It's pretty hilarious, if you think like a five year old, which for me, even today, is not a problem.

The Nation's Capitol (finally under the control of conservatives, thank God. Everyone except for Bush, that is …)

When I was younger, there was something about DC I found appealing. It's the seat of power, to be sure. And wouldn't it have been cool to be a person of note there? I've since come to find out just the opposite. The last thing you want to be is a person of note. Think how difficult your life can become. I loved seeing all the buildings I'd ever heard about. But when I went to the Smithsonian, I was disappointed.

The only cool part was seeing the sarcophagus were Smithson's bones lay. That was more fascinating than looking at dino bones. Putting Smithson back together and hanging him up somewhere … now, that I would pay to see.

Driving in DC is not my favorite thing, although having Texas plates does cause a minor sensation from time to time. It happened in New Jersey, too. I think folks still believe it's the Wild West or something. I don't know if they ever discover the truth, which is that when it's hot, we all try to find a nice place for a cold martini, just like everyone else with any sense.

We stayed at a hotel on Embassy Row. I tried to get the kids to identify the flags that were flying, and they did a pretty good job. I mean, if you guess Afghanistan enough times, you are bound to be right once. But in truth, I have unusually well-informed babies: who's Vice President? Who's

Secretary of State? Who are our Texas Senators? Why is Clinton a disgrace? My kids can answer these questions.

We found the hotel. The staff met my kids … and gave us a great room. I was beginning to think I should have my babies making bets for me someplace, because they were paying off like a slot machine. Maybe I could start to like them, after all. Maybe even earn back that Beanie Baby money I spent. I thought of asking Al to front me some money … until I remembered his overall business policies. I know he'd make the terms extortionate, like five points over the "vig." And he probably would have used those words exactly. He understands money, what can I say? The little, sawed-off Shylock.

Look, the first time you see all those flags flying over the various buildings, you're sitting in Washington, you're a key player in world affairs, you think of all the history in that place, and it gets you a little excited. When I was first there and saw all those countries represented, I knew I had to do something involving exposure to other cultures, at least travel there and soak it all up. I didn't care where it was. Which brings me to the next chapter.

Chapter Five

How I Traveled All Over the World, in Spades, Baby, and Learned to Love It. A Sometimes Hilarious Adventure, Usually at My Own Expense.

I clearly recall my first trip overseas, it was to England. I lived in California and was in New York City on business, so I left from there. I landed at Heathrow very late at night. I didn't book a room, and nothing was available. OK, I'll figure something out. Someone told me to go to Victoria Station and look around there. My plan was to spend the night in London and travel to the south of England: Dover, Arundel, Hastings, just to say I'd been there; another "invasion" of a sort. I went to Victoria Station and noticed *a lot* of people sleeping on the floor, the benches, and the street, everywhere I looked. I thought the Brits had a pretty liberal policy related to homeless people (this was well before homelessness became a cause célèbre).

Lesson #11 in Life

When a celebrity embraces something, be afraid.

Interesting note: Dallas wanted to build a homeless shelter that would cost a little over 3.0 million dollars. By the time it was put it to a vote, the cost was 23.0 million dollars. At least 250,000 homeless people were needed for this type of expense – which was approved — to make sense. But barely 250,000 homeless people live in the entire United States. Dallas, regardless of what we're told, probably has about 1,000 homeless people, if that. With all the money we're spending to salve our irrational guilt, we could put them all up in the new Ritz-Carlton with a full-time nurse and probably save money. God helps those that help themselves, that was written by Ben Franklin over 200 years ago. Government is incompetent almost 99% of the time. You do the math.

Back at Victoria Station, after about 15 minutes one of the guys, fully appointed in Scottish traditional dress (kilts, scarves, etc.) stood up (sort of) and started clapping his hands. About 300 other similarly dressed Scotsmen stood and joined in. I asked a nice lady what was going on, and she responded that these were, what would be called today, the precursors of soccer hooligans. A soccer game was scheduled between England and Scotland, which explained why there was not a single room in the entire city. These guys weren't homeless; they were drunk as all get-out and waiting to party. I had a lot in common with these common folk. Later, when I had time to reflect, they reminded me a lot of Americans: not snobby, just hanging out, regular people. Someone even died from drink, I was told, on the train coming down. This was a scenario not too far removed from our own American experience.

I started chatting up the lady who had answered my question. (I was becoming an Englishman. I no longer "talked" to someone, I chatted them up. In 5 seconds, I was already pretending to be the Duke of Windsor). Her name was Glynnis (ain't they all?). She was about ten years older than I, and she was returning from a single's vacation in Majorca (so far, so good). She was cute, too, and had the cute accent. She told me that we had no hope of finding a place to stay.

"What should we do?" I asked.

"We could break into my daughter's flat since she wouldn't be home until tomorrow afternoon," she suggested.

"No, I don't think that's a great idea, Glynnis. With my current luck, I'll get thrown in jail for breaking and entering." (I could mentally visualize the headlines, above the fold: "American Thief Arrested for B and E." For more on the story, turn to page four.)

"Well," she said, "we could go over to Piccadilly Circus and hang out there 'til morning."

Piccadilly Circus: I was in England, for sure! I took my first ride in a London taxi (great), went by Westminster (Poets' Corner!) and rode by Number 10 Downing Street. Not bad for the first couple of hours in England.

We decided to stop at a Wimpy Burger Bar, sort of a low-rent Burger King. The place was packed with Scotsmen. But first I asked her what the heck a Wimpy burger was. I ordered a Wimpy Giant, which by American standards was really like a Whopper Junior; not really a challenge to a red-blooded, American burger eater like myself. I told the waitress to ask "her," referring to Glynnis, what "she" wanted. Glynnis looked at me like I had three heads.

"What's wrong?," I asked.

"Who's 'her'?" she inquired.

Even to a muddle-head like me, I knew this wasn't good. In a voice somewhat softer, though not totally non-existent, I said, "You, Glynnis."

She looked at me for a second (seemed like an hour), and she finally said, "Keith, you will kindly refer to me as the "Lady," not as an impersonal pronoun."

I swallowed.

I swallowed again.

I said she was totally right, and I've seldom made that error in etiquette in the 30 years since. She wasn't the slightest bit rude but, in point of fact, why shouldn't I refer to a lady this way?

The waitress delivered the burger and soda with no ice. I picked it up and started eating. After about a minute, I saw a camera flash. Glynnis had taken my picture, and I asked her why.

"Because, Keith, we eat beef burgers with a knife and fork."

"Oh," I said, my mouth full, with a little bit of wilted lettuce hanging from the corner. I understood two things about England pretty quickly:

1) their *beef* burgers and tired fries were awful and

2) eating with a knife and fork is all very polite, while you rape and pillage the world for 500 years.

This is a brand of hypocrisy I'd truly come to love.

"So Keith, what brings you to the UK?"

"Oh, it was something I always wanted to do. Sightseeing, mostly. And you, Glynn, did I hear you say you were on a Single's vacation?"

"Yes, I was."

"But you have a daughter?"

"Yes, I was married a very long time ago. I met a Polish man who was living in London. He spoke very little English. I married him and then got divorced not long after. Once he learned to speak the language, I found he wasn't all that interesting."

"I'm sorry to hear that."

"I'm not."

I came to learn later, here and in my travels, that this was a lot of personal information from someone I'd basically just met.

It was about 5:00 in the morning and, all efforts to the contrary, I was getting slightly delirious at this point. Glynnis was taking the train to Birkenhead, which left from Euston Station in a short time. She asked what I was going to do. My original plan was to go to the south of England, but it seems those plans went up in flames.

"I'll go to Euston with you, and I'll just pick somewhere to go." (My luck in doing spontaneous things like this would hold forever.)

When we got to Euston, I looked at this big "clicking" board with a million destinations. Glynn was going north, so I decided to go north. York looked good; I'd read *Richard III*, and this was his "House." I asked one of the Bobbies standing nearby what he thought. He said he was from there and it was worth seeing. (I think he was little appalled at the spontaneity of my plan and in England, where I seemed to do this a lot, it would happen again.) So, Glynn and I made plans to meet in Chester, an old Roman city, in a couple of days. In the meantime, I was off to York.

I had a first class rail pass. The station appeared empty at this hour of the morning. I found my train and found a cabin, seating six, but had it entirely to myself. I started to relax a little bit for the first time in about 24 hours. The weather was very nice, and with this I was extraordinarily lucky. I looked out the window, took out my rail pass and realized I hadn't signed it. I didn't have a pen, either. I got up reluctantly, since I'd have preferred to lay there like a lox.

I went to the cabin next door and knocked, since I'd heard someone in there. A very feminine voice told me to come in (I am not making this up). Upon entering, I beheld one of the prettiest, well-scrubbed, fresh-faced, blonde-headed English women I'd ever seen (I was beginning to *really love* England). I sucked back all the saliva in my mouth, since it had started to flood the instant I saw her and I would have ended up drooling all over my windbreaker, if I hadn't. (After all was said and done later, drooling would have at least been more dignified.)

I said I was sorry for having disturbed her, especially when I noticed the "linebacker in a trench coat" sitting opposite her giving me a look that could freeze my spinal fluid. He wasn't real happy to see me and, I must admit, I wasn't real happy to see him either ... the crumb.

I apologized for having barged in and backpedaled a little, literally, for having done so. I said I thought I heard her say come in. I was also trying to back out the door without banging my head or embarrassing myself any further.

She said, (I am not making this up), "Angel, what do you need?"

I thought this: well, someone wake me from this dream where I'm in a tiny train cabin with a Sissy Spacek look-a-like (it was 1978, after all) who actually appeared to be interested in me (don't forget, I was delirious) and a big caliber gun to take care of "Trench Coat Boy," if he makes any trouble.

But what I said was, "Uh, do you have a pen, by chance?" I'm not making this up; I really said it. It seemed so downright stupid, considering the circumstances. My voice sounded like a five-year-old's because my vocal cords were strung like piano wire, and I was still salivating like Pavlov's dog.

A pen?

I'm sitting:

playing kissy face with Ingrid Bergman,

with a bottle of Dom Pérignon,

at the Pierre Hotel, in New York,

and I want to know if Ingrid has a pen?

That's what it felt like…

I didn't say, "Yeah, baby, you and me. Uh huh. That's what I am talking about. Yeah."

Instead, I said,

"Do you have a pen?"

The next time I find myself with a scantily dressed Kristin Davis walking towards me, with the faint hope of having the pleasure of just *leaning on me* … I'm going to ask her if she wants a sandwich.

My life was in ruins around me.

"George, give him a pen." George obeyed, albeit reluctantly. He was still giving me the "frozen spine" look. For a second I was afraid he was going to *stab me* with the pen instead of handing it to me. I took it and went back to my cabin as fast as my little shaking legs could carry me.

I signed the rail pass and waited for the train to leave. I gazed out the window. And then the magic happened …

"Trench Coat Boy" got off the train – without his pen — and we started to pull out of the station. I couldn't help but notice that the "Love Goddess" hadn't gotten off with him, only the "TCB." Things were indeed looking up. I started to give him the "what for" thru the window, but I remembered how reptiles have eyes that see behind them and I didn't want to get killed over some chick I just met. Or lose my eyeballs, just *this* minute. Chivalry could wait. And to be honest, I was way too tired to have to run for my life. I felt compelled, morally, don't you know, to return the pen to its semi-rightful owner, and I was feeling like a very moral fellow, especially when it would be so utterly self-serving.

I knocked on the door, wiped the drool from my chin with the back of my hand, and awaited her beckoned call. The lady told me to come in. I opened the door and told the lady I wanted to give the lady her pen back (yes, I really said it, again like any other *kindergartener*, and what was my obsession with pens, all of a sudden?). I started to leave and as I did, I asked her if she was going to York.

No. The lady was going to Newark.

I asked if that was before York or after.

The lady said before, and why don't I come up and share the cabin with her?

There is a God.

I took about three milliseconds to get my backpack and take my place next to her "blessedness," this "Venus di Milo" with arms. She was of medium height, slim, wearing skin tight jeans, high leather boats and a knitted clinging sweater that served to complement her figure quite nicely, thank you. Yowsah! Glynnis who?

It was about two hours from her stop in Newark. She chatted while I tried to put coherent, particularly cool sentences together and failed miserably. I asked what she did for a living.

"I work as a hostess in a bar."

"Oh."

"That fellow I was with is a policeman."

"Oh." I was driving *myself* crazy. "I could tell by the trench coat. Have you been doing it long?"

"Yes. Just yesterday we had a rich Arab come in who was dissatisfied with his date or something and caused quite a commotion."

"Dissatisfied with his date?"

"Yes, it was one of the girls who works as a waitress."

"Oh." Can you believe me? All these years later and *I still can't believe me.* "She's a ... waitress?"

"Yes. And I'm the hostess."

There comes a time in every simpleton's life when he graduates from idiot to semi–intelligent, and this was one of them. Janet was a "pro," and the cop was her friendly vice officer. Even I could figure that out (and lucky for me, British cops aren't armed, right?).

"Will you be in the UK long?," she asked me.

"I think about a week. I'm going to spend a day or two in York, then Chester, then back to London."

"I live in London and would love to see you."

Are you kidding me? I'm canceling the rest of my itinerary.

But let me add something. I've never engaged the services of a professional woman in my life. I thought I'd try one once in Amsterdam ... until I saw how they merchandised themselves.[xii] I was also heavily into disillusioning myself: I have to love a person to make love to them. And if I didn't feel the love coming back, I was wasting my time. In essence, what was I really thinking? And real love takes more time than I had.

"Well Janet, I'd very much like to see you (and your legs). Why don't we meet for lunch?"

Lunch? You can't make this up. A "pro" wants to give me a freebie, and I'm asking if she wants bangers and mash. I was beyond hopeless.

"Oh, that would be lovely. But don't call before noon, since I sleep 'til then."

As she was leaving the train, she turned and said to me, "Now Keith, if you don't call me, I should be very disappointed."

I did meet Janet later in London. I called at 12:01 pm. We arranged to meet at Harrod's, and I took Janet out to lunch, fed the lady the first chef salad she had ever had, and then went to Buckingham Palace to watch the changing of the Guard.

Then something very moving happened, which I've never forgotten. First, let me say I am so naïve I really had no clear idea Janet worked that side of the street until my brain fully formed and it became obvious looking back in time. The lady, as far as her interaction with me, was anything but a tramp. She was, in fact, quite sincere, completely open, and totally genuine. Maybe we were kindred spirits when she didn't have to be on guard. I'm told I have an honest face, and maybe it appealed to her. Janet was nothing like the hard cases I've come to realize work in that profession.

As we sat watching the Guard (the band was playing "Close to You"), we sat on a bench, leaned our backs together, and just watched.

We didn't say a word.

We just sat.

It was an intimate moment, without being prurient. I wouldn't experience another moment like it until I met my wife. The difference was that with Janet, it lasted only as long as we sat together. With my bride, it's gone on for these many years.

Janet and I, then, just liked being together. But for all my bold thinking, I had no intention whatsoever of sleeping with her. It would probably be safe to say she wasn't looking to sleep with me, either. It wasn't necessary. We shared, if even for a moment, something much more impactful. Had we ended up in bed together, so be it. There was no hurry. This is how unfeigned attraction *can* work.

We said goodbye and said we'd really miss each other. I meant it, and I think, in fact, know, she meant it, too. We shared something much deeper, yet very simple: a genuine emotional connection.

I knew I had to be going. It was getting near dusk, and I had a train to catch, both to where I was staying and, of course, ultimately back to America. I didn't want to go. I felt so comfortable, with someone essentially a stranger, though a different kind than I, at that moment. I looked at her for a long moment, for as long as I could. I wanted to remember her face. I hugged her gently and kissed her cheek. I looked in her blue eyes one last time. She smiled at me, and I left. She'd understood.

And I never looked back.

I often wondered what had happened to Janet.

I went to Chester, Liverpool, crossed the Mersey River, looking for Gerry and The Pacemakers. Romance, or the chance for it, seemed to seek me out during this trip (and no other that I recall).

How I got to Chester is quite a story in itself. At the B and B where I was staying, there was an elderly couple – American – who were staying there, also. They had a car and asked if I'd like to go with them. That, of course, should have been my first clue (s): old, retired, and driving on the left. Not a good combination. Calling the ultimate trip hair-raising would have been a *gross understatement.* The fact that we ended up anywhere *near* Chester was a miracle, no less than the fishes and loaves and worthy of celebration.

I had the gabadootz scared out of me more times than one can imagine. No experience gets the old cardio system going quite like ending up in the right lane, like in America, and having a semi bearing down on you at incredible speed while blasting his horn. I say it *looked* really fast because, at this point and the *75 other times* it happened during a *100 kilometer* trip, I was horizontal in the back seat, crying my eyes out, and praying to anyone who would listen. I would have worshipped Baal, if I thought it would have gotten me through this trip faster. These folks were kind of deaf, so they didn't hear my screams of desperation; they just thought the whole experience was "exciting." No, Janet was exciting. This was a bloodcurdling, hair-raising, labored-breathing, harrowing. It was not exciting in the sense I've ever used that word. It's like saying Hiroshima was just a family barbeque. This type of experience is not good for anyone over 50, and these folks were 150. They could not have lived much longer after that road trip. My own life expectancy, I'm sure, was reduced by about a third. Technically, I should be dead.

Dateline: Chester, England

(Where I did a walking tour with Mr. Douglas, who looked exactly like Alfred Hitchcock)

I stayed in a hotel that was 350 years old and used to be a stop on the coach trail to London. The ticket window still existed, and it was the window to the bar, which I loved. I rendezvoused with Glynnis. "The Lady" took me to see

"Huckleberry Finn" set to music at a place called the Every-man Playhouse in Liverpool. Considering they were Brits, they did a great job capturing the essence of the novel: basically, that racism is evil. Huck clearly understood that when he said he may have to sacrifice his life in order to let Jim go. This was well before "Big River" came to Broadway, but maybe putting that spectacular novel to music had been in the works for several years. I don't know.

G and I went to a large Victorian restaurant for a night-cap. The place was gigantic. We cozied up to the bar and sipped our drinks. I stood there thinking I was in England, in a place I'd never thought I would ever be (the home of the Beatles) with a strikingly attractive woman, just hanging out. What can I say? I leaned over and kissed her. How could I not? She kissed back, also. She asked me if I fell easily. I was stunned only because, at that moment, she clearly had my number. Not a position I love being in. I didn't know what to say, so we kissed again.

I realized later that there was nothing exotic about this interlude at all for the lady. The lady was at home. Not being the least of it, the lady probably saw Americans all the time. Nothing happened, and I eventually left. She was a terrific lady whom I remember very fondly. I never saw her again. On the way home that night on the train, I was solicited by a very aggressive homosexual. It took about 15 minutes before I realized the guy was gay. He should have been wearing a sandwich board or something. I am such a man of the world, right? I had effectively gone from the sublime to the utterly ridiculous, within the course of 24 hours. Now that's irony, my friends.

I left for London, with a stop in Birmingham. I was walking through the outdoor market when I tripped and, on the way down, I accidentally grabbed a handful of the woman's hindquarters in front of me. She was about to scream MASHER! when I scurried back onto the train, sweating ever so slightly.

Before I got to London, I took a quick side trip to Stratford. As every English-majoring fool can tell you, you have to make your pilgrimage to the Master's final resting place. It took a while to get there, and when I finally did, I was held back by a rope about 30 feet away from Shakespeare's grave. I stood there with the other tourists and felt somewhat short-changed. This was, to me, a little unjust. I'd come a long way and, narcissist that I am, I thought I deserved better. I went over to the guard and explained my predicament. After all, what did I have to lose? He lowered the rope and let in only me. I couldn't believe it. I didn't turn around to see how the others responded. Maybe they thought I was a cancer patient or something doing my version of a trip to Lourdes. This was incredibly lucky for me. I communed in the holy atmosphere until I felt satisfied and had not worn out this man's generosity in letting me make my hajj. I went out the other way, still reeling from this fabulous fortune that had befallen me. I never forgot how nice this man had been to me.

Dateline: Windsor Castle

Before I met Janet, I'd arranged to stay in Windsor, thinking I could take the train back and forth from London. I also booked a room in advance, so I wouldn't wind up on the street again (though it had served me quite well, hadn't it?). When I arrived, I picked up the info about the room and directions on how to get there. As I walked, I saw that the castle and grounds take up a large part of the town and are hard to miss unless you were Stevie Wonder or something. I kept getting closer to the castle, looking for my room. I'd finally gotten to the last brownstone, if you will, right by the side gates. Surely, this couldn't be it; I had to be wrong. I looked around and knocked on the door, the door knocker being one of those "clangor type" things.

As I stood on the front step, the door opened and one of the most gorgeous creatures I had ever seen answered the door and asked if I was Mr. Price. She looked like Elizabeth Hurley. All I said was, like Ralph Kramden, "Hum – in – a, Hum – in – a, Hum – in – a." She took that as a "yes."

"Please come in," she said. "We were getting worried about you. Let me show you your room."

We ascended the stairs to the third floor, and she gave me her son's room. You should have seen how nicely appointed that house was. If I had a lot of money, I'd choose to live there, which I can't say about the run of the mill B and B, though the ones I stayed in were quite nice. But *this* was Park Avenue. Her son's room looked like a young guy's room: posters, stereo, books. I felt like an intruder and told her I couldn't possibly stay there. She told me not to worry; he was away at cooking school … learning how to make the two dishes the British can barely make. OK, I made up that last part, but he was away at cooking school, and I don't even want to know the core curriculum around 1978 (bangers and mash, fried fish, veal pie … is that it?). Breakfast was at 7:30, if that was OK, or when I could get there.

When I got up in the morning, I went down to the dining room, while this nice lady served me off silver and china. I had to be in a parallel universe or something, because this was more like a Ritz-Carlton and cost about $15 USD, in those easy times.

Later in the trip, I became friendly with this gorgeous woman and asked, with all due respect, how a woman with abundant means like she clearly had, would open a B and B. It couldn't be because the lady craved meeting new people, i.e. obnoxious tourists. The lady told me she had gotten divorced and things change, right? I had to admire that, since it couldn't have been easy. We hung out and drank tea in the private kitchen. I felt privileged because this was not an offer the lady made casually, I learned later. This was a very classy woman. I would have asked her for a date, had I had any sense and didn't consider her at least 15 atmospheres above my station on earth. She was terrific. I went back years later and tried to see her, but she was out of town. Maybe next time.[xiii]

Meanwhile, Back Home at the French Bistro in DC ...

It was dinner time, and we were situated among about 100 places to eat. Different cuisines were available, and we chose a French bistro. We didn't get the reception I usually get when someone meets my kids. The staff were standoffish ... and they were French, too. I could learn to hate these people who treat me like dirt and then take my money, which is a core part of their belief system, it appears.

But I had a victory to win here, because I had a secret weapon (s): my kids and their consummate knowledge of good food, prepared professionally. I cook all the time and have really gotten quite good: Cajun, Italian, down home American. In a word, I have basically spoiled the beejeebees out of them. No chicken nuggets and hot dogs they. This was what Pierre, the snobby waiter and little Brie Eater, was about to find out. He'd end up loving us, if my plans worked as expected. By the way, as punishment for Germany after

World War 2, we should have made them *keep France*. Just to mess with them both, in perpetuity.

Any way, "Frog Boy" seated us at a lousy table, right by the entrance. I was getting torked, but not enough to make a scene … yet. I still had a wagon to fix. I ordered a martini to see if the pinhead could make one. This means a small glass like you see in the old movies where the olive takes up about a third. This guarantees that the drink will stay cold to the bottom, which is key, isn't it? Bigger ain't always better, especially when it comes to the most beautiful drink in the world.

So, "DeGaulle" brings me the drink. Not too bad. He gave my kids the fancy French menu (in French, which my daughter speaks, so nice try, Waterloo Boy).

"Toad Stool" – Alex — read the menu, (which was bigger than he was), and said "The tenderloin of beef, how is it prepared?"

Why don't I ever have a movie camera around when I need one?

Seeing the look of utter amazement on Frenchie's face was worth the price of the dinner. A photo of that classic "spit take" should have wound up in the Smithsonian as a national treasure, with the caption, "PEANUT-SIZED AMERICAN SURPRISES AND HUMILIATES SNOBBY FRENCH WAITER, AVENGING THOUSANDS. Story on page 2."

It was that beautiful. But there was more ….

"Medium," and then he added, "sir."

"OK," Al said. "And I'll start with the Caesar salad."

At this point, Bordeaux Boy looked like he was gagging up a cotton ball.

"And you … Miss?"